Wall Stenciling

YESTERDAY'S SKILLS
ADAPTED TO TODAY'S MATERIALS

Wall Stenciling

Richard M. Bacon

Camden, Maine

◆

Dedicated to
a pair of modern artists,
DAVID AND GERARD WIGGINS,
who carry on the Yankee tradition of self-reliance

© 1991 by Richard M. Bacon

Cover and text design by Amy Fischer, Camden, Maine
Cover and interior photographs by Ralph Copeland, Thomaston, Maine
Typeset by Camden Type 'n Graphics, Camden, Maine
Printed and bound in the United States

Library of Congress Cataloging-in-Publication Data
Bacon, Richard M.
    Wall stenciling / by Richard M. Bacon
        p.   cm. — (The Forgotten arts)
    Includes bibliographical references
    ISBN 0-89909-326-4
    1. Stencilwork—United States.   I. Title.   II. Series.
NK8662.B3   1991
745.7'3—dc20   91-11560
                                                          CIP

10   9   8   7   6   5   4   3   2   1

Contents

	Preface	vii
	Acknowledgments	ix
	Introduction	1
ONE	The Tradition of Stenciled Walls in New England	8
TWO	Elements and Origins of Wall Stencil Designs	21
THREE	Consider Design and Color	35
FOUR	The Mechanics of Stenciling	46
FIVE	Laying Out a Wall	68
	APPENDIX A Painted and Stenciled Floors	79
	APPENDIX B A Portfolio of Stencil Designs	95
	Further Reading	115
	Notes on Supplies	117

Preface

The Age of Recycling is upon us. It grabs the headlines as we race to readjust priorities—to save our planet and ourselves. While not a new conception, it speaks today with an increasing, often desperate, urgency.

Generations of New Englanders have traditionally recycled things—saving bits of this and that with the prospect of devising something better. This frugal outlook still persists. Look in anybody's attic or garage today. Historically it became a way of life to help settlers survive and prosper in a new and often inhospitable land where ready cash was hard to come by. Before long the Yankee dictum, "Use it up, wear it out, make it do, do without," was so deeply ingrained it was sometimes seen as a character flaw rather than the strength it is. And not surprisingly this attitude was part of the mental baggage that was carried West as the country expanded and developed. In many pockets of our society, recycling has always been a viable philosophy.

But as this book demonstrates, Yankees also recycled *ideas*. Wall stenciling is one of them: a marriage of Yankee thrift and creativity. When they saw something they liked—and thought they could not afford—they figured out how to duplicate it by using materials at hand and relying on their talent.

Although creativity is a universal gift, many rural home-owners who were hard-pressed keeping up with changing urban fashion hired itinerant journeymen to decorate walls and floors with stenciled patterns. The more adventurous among them either copied or adapted what they admired. The work of a special few reflects their own individual tastes and abilities.

The Wiggins brothers, David and Gerard, are part of this Yankee tradition by inheritance, by temperament, and by choice. Their work as decorative artists for more than two and a half decades has led them, separately and together, to study old methods of wall stenciling and investigate new products and techniques. Many times they have gone beyond early nineteenth century wall stenciling and what is now known as the traditional New England "country" look of Moses Eaton. They have applied their own talents toward developing period and modern wall decorations that are surprisingly contemporary.

To them the author is indebted for their inspiration and selfless guidance—twice over.

Acknowledgments

The author wishes to thank the following people for their graciousness in allowing him to intrude upon their lives during the preparation of this edition of this book:

- Foremost are the brothers David and Gerard Wiggins and their wives.
- For allowing us to photograph their houses, we are also indebted to:

  Mr. Jacob Atwood, Mr. and Mrs. Brad Atwood
  Mr. and Mrs. Courtland Freese
  Mr. and Mrs. George Roberts
  Mr. and Mrs. Robert O. Stuart
  Mr. Douglas Towle

• For the bulk of photography, the author is indebted to Mr. Ralph Copeland, of course, and for the use of additional photographs to:

Mr. Ronnie Newman
Mr. Gerard Wiggins

This book originally appeared in 1977 under the title *The Art and Craft of Wall Stenciling,* with photography by David Asgard, and was published by Funk & Wagnalls, New York. The author is indebted to Harper & Row, Publishers, for reverting the rights to the author so that he could rewrite large portions of it and include current information for this *Forgotten Arts* edition by Yankee Books.

Introduction

In this country, wall stenciling began as a rural New England
phenomenon in the early nineteenth century and quickly
burgeoned as news of the current trend in home decoration
spread from village to farm across the land. In that first flush of
acceptance, the craze reached as far west as Ohio and south to the
Middle Atlantic states. Then in the 1840s it died its first death.
Stenciling was replaced by the thing it had originally set out to
copy—wallpaper.

Since only the wealthy could import wallpapers from Europe, Yankee ingenuity came into play soon after the American
Revolution when artisans devised ways to create the effect of
wallpaper without the expense: they applied paint through patterned cutouts directly to a plastered or sheathed wall.

This method of repeating design motifs and running borders was a quick, adaptable, and simple way of imitating what many rural homeowners could not afford. It also satisfied their need for color and pattern and—in many cases where they did it themselves—a universal craving for self-expression. Those same needs exist today.

News of the latest fashions in home decoration spread largely by word of mouth in the early days of our country and by the varying abilities of itinerant craftsmen whose geographic progress through sparsely populated areas can still be traced by the walls they left behind. Stenciling was pervasive, even though its greatest popularity spanned only about three and a half decades. But newly stenciled walls continued to be laid out for decades longer in isolated houses and taverns beyond the fringes of established settlements as the population expanded westward.

Today authentic examples are still being discovered by proud homeowners who start a new renovation project only to find a buried treasure from yesterday gradually unfolding before their eyes. Often these decorations are lovingly preserved despite changing tastes and the ravages of time—the cracked and flaking plaster, the faded colors, and the inevitable water stains.

Even the most distressed wall today evokes a feeling of nostalgia for what is thought to have been a simpler, quieter era. In the best preserved examples, one senses a harmony, an integrity, and a freedom of expression that are infectious and almost magical.

By the 1840s, however, interest in wall stenciling started to ebb. Factories in New England began to produce a wide range of printed patterns on cheap paper. Homemakers could then buy these in long rolls. Usually they came in overall designs and were sold with coordinating strips for running borders to paste along the top of the wall. These wallpapers were easily applied over the work of the early craftsmen and, as individual tastes changed or the colors faded, it was acceptable for successive generations to keep adding layer upon layer of wallpaper.

Many antique houses with original stenciled walls no longer stand today or, if they do, they have been so overlayered with

Even the ravages of time have not completely obliterated this stenciled wall in The Temperance Tavern (1793) in Gilmanton, New Hampshire. Here an unknown itinerant combined an all-over pattern with architectural and classical references while exercising his own individuality.

paper or paint it is hard to realize how pervasive the art of wall stenciling was in the years before the Civil War.

Perhaps most readers have never actually seen a stenciled room that was done in the early nineteenth century, but there are enough private homes left—as well as many research books and whole sections of walls and sheathing that museums have salvaged and put on public display—to show the widespread acceptance of this early type of home decoration during its golden age. They also testify to its appeal.

During later periods when there was a trend for more obvious formality, wall stenciling made a brief comeback with motifs suggested by Old World designs, particularly from Greece and Rome. Oftentimes, in larger rooms with higher ceilings, only a stenciled frieze was applied at the top of the wall. Sometimes

Although the frieze has faded, there is still magic in this panel—a combination of strong vertical borders and sinuous vines—that was stenciled in four colors by the same itinerant known only as "The Boarder."

running borders were added around window and door frames, too, but large areas of negative space to which a tinted wash had been applied were left to give visitors a feeling of openness and elegance.

In rooms where a sense of more intimacy was wanted, an all-over pattern (the closest to a manufactured wallpaper design but different from earlier stenciled ones where simple repeated motifs floated within regularly spaced panels) tended to close in the space and make it more cozy. This kind of decoration was often used in bedrooms.

Still, it is the earlier nineteenth century stencil designs—the ones that used motifs like pineapples, leaves, flowers, sunbursts, and other geometric patterns within a series of panels—that have become most firmly established in the public mind as creating the authentic "country" look. Sometimes primitive, and often placed intuitively with little regard for symmetry, this is a New England decorating classic which seems both homey and free-spirited. It is the kind most sought today by those intent on recreating the ambiance of a bygone era while still keeping both feet in the present.

In one of its latest resurrections, wall stenciling was embraced by rural homemakers in the 1970s with the same dedicated zeal that coincided with the back-to-the-land movement of that era and a rebirth of interest in post-and-beam houses, herbs, natural foods, alternative lifestyles, and the pursuit of self-sufficiency. Today it is still running its course in the suburbs as appropriate background for collections of early American artifacts and furniture.

Wall stenciling is a *mechanical* process. It is achieved by applying paint through holes cut in a semi-rigid material and is the same method still used today to label packing crates. There are some limitations inherent in the process itself but, once the design and colors are chosen, stenciling is an inexpensive way of repeating the same patterns over and over quickly and efficiently.

Yet it can be a *creative* process as well. Anyone can take traditional patterns and copy them. Many can adapt and refine them. A few can create original designs that are altogether different and—by arranging them in exciting ways, by delving into the fascinating study of color and its effects, by taking a fresh look at shapes and spatial relationships—come up with a unique interpretation with this mechanical approach to decorating a wall or floor.

Today's wall stencilers use modern products and paints to carry on an art form that was popular soon after this nation was founded. As homeowners create new interiors, they are also recreating the spirit of initiative and individual choice that has disappeared from so many aspects of modern life.

This original leafy frieze was created by David Wiggins for a girl's bedroom. It is sparingly combined with more traditional borders and then lightly overpainted with a freehand brush.

There have always been craftsmen in isolated pockets of every culture who continue to practice the old ways despite changing times. But there are also those who can adapt old techniques, experiment with new products, and infuse their work with a modern spirit. David and Gerard Wiggins are two of them, for their work is continuing to evolve.

A stenciled wall or patterned floor may remind us today of an era when every man wanted to be his own master and often was, of a time when both men and women knew how to do many things well because they had to. Perhaps the spirit of those times can teach us now that artistic creativity is not the sole domain of the expert as it so often seems today.

The purpose of this book is not to recapture the flavor of a forgotten art and leave it at that. Nor is it solely to show how old techniques can be adapted to a modern age by anyone with a will. Rather, it is to encourage the reader to experiment with personal, inborn talents. Herein lies one path to real freedom and a road that anyone can safely travel.

CHAPTER ONE

The Tradition of
Stenciled Walls in New England

Stenciling as an easy device to produce repeated patterns has been traced to many different cultures. Apparently, it was one of those simultaneously developed crafts that were common to widely separated peoples. The early Chinese used the stencil to decorate caves and manuscripts. The Japanese stenciled fabrics and screens. Primitive peoples in the Pacific islands decorated their clothing with stenciled designs. On the other side of the world the Egyptians patterned tombs and burial artifacts, the Greeks stenciled pottery borders, and the early Romans taught boys to write using stenciled letters.

During the Middle Ages, stenciling flourished under the guidance and encouragement of the Church—through religious texts and music scores, image pictures, banners, and holy decoration within the church itself. In France stencils, combined with woodblock prints, were used to overlay colors on manuscripts, playing cards, and wall hangings. Political manifestos and broadsides were commonly stenciled in the days before the printing press. Squares of paper covered with repeated designs—an idea brought back by travelers to ancient China—were pasted on interior walls to imitate expensive tapestries and woven fabrics of intricate design.

But in the American wilderness—far from the centers of fashion—settlers had little means and even less time to spend on expensive decoration. Their lives were directed toward subsis-

New England winters were cold even with the Indian shutters drawn and a fire going. This cross-hatch stencil design within a now faded border must have helped lighten the spirits.

tence, to establishing themselves and their families on inland farms, clearing and cultivating land, setting up mills and businesses, cooperating with their neighbors to build meetinghouses and schools. There was not enough time from dawn to long after dark to reflect on changing tastes and new fads of decoration. There was not even enough time to accomplish all that had to be done just to exist as one season slid into the next. Change came slowly to hard-working countrymen and women.

One refinement that paved the way for change in their homes, however, was the shift from interior wood sheathing and paneling to plastered walls. By the middle of the 1700s, plaster was in general use. Until then thrifty Yankees had made the most of native materials and, of these, wood was the most abundant. Even the wood-paneled fireplace wall was beginning to give way to plaster in houses built after 1800.

Plastered walls helped lighten the interiors of colonial houses. Windows were small and economically spaced, because glass was expensive and difficult to replace. New England winters were raw and threatening, and the town assessors had developed the custom of levying taxes on the amount of glass in a citizen's house. Plaster also created a seamless surface that resulted in large areas of wall surface that were easier to keep clean—a consideration that was important when houses were heated with wood and before the development of effective screening.

Early plaster made with lime and cow or horse hair was certainly better than wood in many ways, but it usually dried gray. To increase the light, countrymen coated their plastered walls with whitewash or "distemper" (a mixture of water, glue, and coloring). Color was needed to lift the spirits in a northern environment that seemed covered with snow a great part of the year or—if not for as long as they imagined—reflected only the dull tans and browns of between seasons until summer finally brought visual relief and escape to the outdoors.

Some of the popular tints in those early days were red or yellow ochers, blues, light greens, and shades of rose. But once they had color, the homesteaders frequently pined for something more—pattern, perhaps, to add interest to their walls. Soon they were primed for the arrival of the journeyman who would not only

News traveled. So did unknown journeymen like the one who combined stenciled urns and swags with a vertical border of flowers in the front hall of The Tavern.

bring them news from the more fashionable urban centers along the coast but could also decorate their walls with patterns in a practical and economical way. This would make them feel a part of progress although living far removed.

Once the wilderness had been tamed, the land was under cultivation, and settlers could think of themselves as members of communities rather than as pioneers, one thing that accelerated the journeyman's arrival was the establishment of a better transportation system after the War of Independence had been fought and won. Roads and canals, turnpikes and stages fanned out greedily along river valleys and through mountain passes, puncturing the isolation of the upland farms. The farmer could now send his produce to urban markets more easily and, with the increased profits, buy manufactured goods that would make his family's life less arduous. Equally important to his wife was that better roads brought more frequent travelers who, in turn, carried news. It was now more possible than before to keep abreast of what was happening beyond the rim of hills.

Long before these developments eased the burden of living on the land, news had filtered to rural areas that current home decoration imported from Europe had been refined for the wealthy. There were two specific developments to account for this during the late 1700s.

One was the importation of French wallpaper. This was highly prized but—because of stiff import duties—very expensive. The purchase and application of printed papers to the interior walls of houses showed not only the means of the upper class but also the fact that the merchant and his family were conversant with European fashion even though living in the Colonies. In a new land there are no cultural traditions, only ties. Ties to Europe were important, especially among the wealthy and educated, for everything European was admired, imported, and talked about.

It was also copied. One of the first to copy wallpaper was Plunkett Fleeson of Philadelphia, who in 1739 made it possible for even the near-wealthy to buy a product made on this side of the Atlantic and thereby avoid paying taxes on it. The use of wallpaper could now spread even further among the sophisticated gentry.

The other development came later in the century. This was the rediscovery of classicism. The four Adam brothers—architects, builders, and designers from Scotland, of whom Robert and James are the most remembered—were employed by the royalty and nobility of England to design and build estates. They turned away from the heaviness of French and Italian design when they discovered and refined the elegance of early Roman and Greek classicism. Theirs was a formal, symmetrical treatment of space that influenced design on both sides of the Atlantic. They used classic columns and fluted pilasters, friezes, readings, and rosettes; placed urns and statuary in arches and niches; and applied plaster and lead ornaments to walls and ceilings.

This stenciled swag of leaves and flowers alternating with drop ornaments might have been suggested by the use of fabrics and their design. It was used as a frieze by David Wiggins.

Wall stencilers took their inspiration mainly from wallpaper designs, which, in turn, had begun to reflect the classical influence of the Adam brothers. Swags and drop ornaments were lifted freely from fabric designs; deep entablatures and flutings imitated plaster or wooden moldings that were not there. So stencil designs—however crude because of their limitations— were devised to imitate these decorations, too.

There is no present evidence that stenciled rooms appeared in early urban centers, although examples of the craft may have been destroyed and never recorded because of the more constant and rapid changes in home decoration there than in the country. The earliest stenciled room that Janet Waring, author of *Early American Stencils on Walls and Furniture*, verified is in the 1778 Goodale Homestead in Marlborough, Massachusetts. Another author, Nina Fletcher Little, in her book *American Decorative Wall Painting (1700–1850)*, states that she saw this type of decoration used as background in an unidentified portrait painted by Joseph Stewart in 1793.

One tradition holds that the art of wall stenciling was first practiced after the Revolution by wandering Hessian soldiers who had brought their craft with them from Europe. Others claim it was the people from the Rhine Valley who practiced the craft when they came to settle in Pennsylvania. There is no scholarly proof that either of these legends is true. Waring believed that the stencil technique as applied to houses came with the English settlers from East Anglia and that the wall designs were the product of the innovative Yankee journeymen—forever intent to turn fashion to profit.

From his own investigation of early nineteenth century stenciling, David Wiggins has found that groups of women—using stencils and employed in a factory situation—decorated chairs and trays. Men stenciled walls. The women did finer work and preferred using a piece of velvet wrapped around a finger to pat the gold and bronze powders into the stencil cutouts; the men generally used blunt-nosed stencil brushes to apply paint to the wall. Of the other folk art of that century, Wiggins adds, more than half was done by women.

There are three major areas in which stenciled rooms from the early 1800s have been found: the southwest corner of Massachusetts, spilling over into Connecticut and New York State; south central Vermont along the Connecticut River and reaching back into the Green Mountains around Plymouth; and southeastern New Hampshire, radiating out from the Merrimack River valley into southern Maine and northeastern Massachusetts.

Spotted thoughout the countryside in homesteads and in taverns, there is still evidence of nineteenth century stencilers' work being uncovered today as old houses undergo restoration and renovation. There is also evidence that much of it is being destroyed where homeowners do not recognize—or do not appreciate—its historical value.

Probably the wandering artisan or peddler—for these were

This unique example of the decorative skills of a 19th century itinerant shows whimsical birds perched under an arch of leaves. It was stenciled on a tinted wall between two windows in the master bedroom of a colonial house—perhaps a bit of folly that interrupted an otherwise symmetrical all-over pattern.

versatile men of many trades—was the first to carry new decorative trends to the countryside. He plied his craft from one community to another—either alone or with an apprentice journeyman—for little more than room and board during the winter months when it was better to be doing indoor work next to the fire than to be caught out on the road.

However, there is good evidence that master craftsmen were

not the only people to decorate lonely farmsteads with patterned walls and floors. Lydia Eldredge Williams of Ashfield, Massachusetts, stenciled five rooms in her house sometime in the early 1800s. It is probable that many of the walls standing today as monuments to the past were also executed by other gifted and self-taught homesteaders who had heard of or seen stenciled rooms and set about to re-create them in their own houses as best they could.

When Waring first began the study of stenciled rooms in the 1920s and 1930s, she uncovered many examples under layers of wallpaper. Some of the houses she recorded were already in the advanced states of deterioration; many have long since disappeared. But often old walls were being preserved even then. They spoke to her as directly and simply as they must have done when they were first stenciled.

The names of some nineteenth century wall stencilers are well known. Some of their stencil patterns are in museum collections and their wanderings are a part of the historical record. But for the most part these journeymen did not sign their work, *per se*, although the colors and patterns they repeated from house to house bear their individual mark. Those interested in establishing the authencity of a particular wall will run into difficulty, unless family records or historical documents note such facts, and most antiquarians must be content with the phrase "attributed to." David Wiggins, for example, attributes many stenciled walls and murals in central New Hampshire to "The Boarder"—a man presumably out of Portsmouth—by distinctive freehand squiggles that embellish some of his stenciled walls and by repeated images in his murals such as uprooted trees, which may have a religious origin.

One of the confusions comes in the repetition of a few popular motifs in widely scattered parts of the country. Stencil patterns are easy to transport and to copy: they can be traced from a wall directly or cut from another stencil. Although one can note variations attributable to the skill of an individual stencil cutter, patterns appear to have been lifted freely from one another, perhaps lent to a fellow journeyman, or taken off by the apprentice when he fulfilled his contract.

However, many stencilers have been identified by the consistency of their work. The motifs, placement, and colors of the Eatons—father and son—continue to be the most widely publicized and appreciated. The Eaton look has become the classic "country" look and is by far the most popular today.

Moses Eaton, Sr., (1753–1833) served in the Revolution and at the age of 40 moved from Needham, Massachusetts, to Han-

This fireplace wall in a 1700s house in Maine includes many of the elements and motifs used by Moses Eaton; however, the patterns were applied recently. This wide spacing and nod to symmetry gives the room its classic country look.

The country look of this dining room in an old house in northern Vermont follows tradition but was actually only stenciled by David Wiggins a few years ago.

cock in southern New Hampshire. His son, Moses, Jr., was born there in 1796 and died at the age of 90. Both were journeymen artists and farmers at some point in their lives—those kinds of men trained to do many things.

Eventually the younger man built a house in the adjoining town of Harrisville, New Hampshire, where he became known for his abilities as a farmer. How much stenciling he did after his move is a matter of speculation. His house no longer stands, but Waring saw and studied it in the 1930s. It was there that a stencil kit—probably used by both father and son—was discovered and later given to the Society for the Preservation of New England Antiquities in Boston. It contained 78 Eaton stencils—which make up 40 complete designs—as well as eight brushes, dry pigments, and chalk. The kit shows more about the methods and work habits of the men than about the art. The stencils had been beveled with a sharp knife to make crisper outlines. Made of heavy paper and coated with oil, many of the patterns are still covered with the soft greens, brick reds, and yellow ochers that have become the hallmark of the Eatons' work. Copies of these stencils are in the print collection of the Metropolitan Museum in New York City.

Moses Eaton, Jr., was known for his alternating and repeating motifs floating within verticle stenciled panels. This was most popular in the 1820 to 1840 period.

Previous to that, it is likely that stenciling had followed the same evolution as wallpaper design that was so far beyond most people's reach. Probably at first, French *domino* papers (the design outlines printed with wooden blocks and the colors overlaid with stencils) had been cut into strips and glued to the wall adjacent to the wood trim and framing as borders to enhance architectural detail—or to create visual interest if detail were missing. These lent the room elegance and formalty. It also left a lot of negative space.

Eaton worked in a period of more—rather than less—pattern. Still, considering what was to evolve later, one cannot call his an all-over conception, which leaves far less unstenciled space than Eaton ever did. However, his work does reflect a strong influence of the wallpaper design of the time: the deep frieze at the top of the wall; the base or surbase borders; regularly spaced verticals to suggest panels; and widely spaced abstract, geometric motifs that float within them. Reedings and stenciled flutings also suggest the classical influence. By the time the Eatons were practicing their craft, the basic components of wall stencil design had already been set.

There were many equally talented and prolific wall stencilers in the past. Some of them were Nathaniel Parker of North Weare, New Hampshire; Rufus Porter of Boxford, Massachusetts (who often combined stenciling with mural painting and wrote a book and many articles about his decorative arts and scientific interests); Henry O. Goodrich, who was born in Nottingham, New Hampshire, and died at the age of 20; Erastus Gates of Plymouth, Vermont, who married into the Coolidge family from whom President Coolidge was descended; and Emery Rice of Hancock, New Hampshire, who traversed much of the same ground as the Eatons but at a later date.

There was even the legendary "Stimp," who worked the lower Berkshires, and The Boarder, who covered walls south of the White Mountains. It has been suggested that Stimp's designs and mechanical precision were often affected by a growing love of alcohol as he worked. And there must have been hundreds more whose work confirms their talent but whose names no one bothered to record.

Wall stenciling remains today what it was from the beginning: a simple and effective way to reproduce design quickly and efficiently. The greater range of materials and paints offered on today's market allow the modern stenciler to work more easily and sometimes more freely. But the attraction of the well-designed and executed antique stenciled wall will remain a part of our folklore and visual history. No matter who the artist, it will continue to cast its spell.

CHAPTER TWO

Elements and Origins of Wall Stencil Designs

The primary challenge for the wall stenciler today is not in mastering the mechanics. With practice and a certain dexterity, these can be learned quickly.

More important at this stage is the time spent investigating what stenciling is all about. This includes its historical components—their relationship and their development. Only by experimenting can you choose suitable designs that will result in a pleasing sense of order. Even with the wide range of personal tastes and abilities involved in any good home decoration, success will ultimately depend on the design elements chosen to create a harmonious environment. For this the key is *order*.

It is perfectly possible to pattern a wall on the basis of whimsey by laying out one design here, another over there, and three or four of a different conception somewhere in between. This, however, will lead to visual chaos rather than satisfy a need for stability. Whimsical decoration can be fun. But without a sense of order—unless you want to live with it permanently or overpaint it later when you tire of quirkiness—the results will remain just that—merely fun. It would be better to plan carefully so you can create a finished product that is more permanent.

Absolute symmetry in a layout is something else. In the work of most early stencilers the placement of design elements was usually predetermined by the architectural features of a room and the measurements of the walls themselves. But there are plenty of examples where one can see—whether through haste to get the job done, or a lack of planning, or some artful instinct at work—that balance has given way to expediency and patterns just don't line up exactly. Often, this asymmetry can be admired because a byproduct of wall stenciling can be a justifiable spontaneity.

If you want to re-create an historical setting, a lot of the work of design has already been done for you even if you don't have access to the work of an earlier stenciler you admire. Many traditional patterns are available in reference books and in museums. You can trace the patterns, measure the distances, duplicate the colors, and reproduce an old wall in a new place by making only slight variations in spacing to fit changed dimensions. There are ways even to make it look old or "distressed" (see Chapter 3), if that is your aim.

Selecting designs from historic patterns and fusing them into a new unity, changing both their color and placement to fit your own surroundings, will be more challenging than any outright duplication. For this you can work from old stencil patterns or from photographs; you can rescale, draw, and cut the traditional designs like those included in Appendix B. This will be more creative—but more time consuming—than buying pre-cut historical patterns that are available on today's market.

Ultimately, however, you may want to create your own de-

The swags in the frieze, the urns in the surbase design, and vertical flower borders all lend elegance to this bedroom in The Temperance Tavern. Note the tinted panels (negative space) and the stenciler's unconcern with absolute symmetry.

sign. For this you must experiment with spatial relations, the interplay of shapes, and the effect of lines. And you must study color. Many of your ideas may have to be discarded before you come up with an overall design whose sense of order is completely satisfying.

Whether you copy or adapt designs from known examples or draw your inspiration from forms in nature, geometry, or some competing decorative art, you will find that all design is somehow derivative. To trace the origins and become familiar with the elements that previous stencilers have found to be successful will be time well spent. Not only will you have a better understanding of some of the problems you face and overcome in this elusive

Elegance and restraint are the keynotes of this parlor in a 1700s New Hampshire house (actually one reconstructed recently from three old houses). The paneled Indian shutters, wainscotting, tinted and stenciled walls all make a fitting background for the owners' collections of American antiques.

search for order, but you will also gain greater satisfaction with the results.

It is obvious that early nineteenth century stencilers were inspired by the designs of wallpapers, for they set out to imitiate them in paint and produce a similar effect at a greatly reduced cost. Because of the restrictions imposed by the stencil itself and the range of colors available, the results were more direct and simpler than wallpapers were. They do not have to be today.

The placement of the motifs, the depth of the borders, the shapes of individual patterns, and even the colors were conventionally accepted standards. This did not preclude variety, however. At its best, good design came from individual creativity; at its worst, through general incompetence even in copying.

Yet wallpaper designs were also derivative. They took their inspiration from fabrics (tassels, swags, folds, repeated or diaper patterns), from architecture (pilasters, medallions, moldings, urns), from nature (leaves, fruits, flowers, birds, shells, nuts), and from geometrical shapes (triangles, circles, shields, stars). Often, designers in all of the arts have been inspired by motifs that are as old as the human race itself and common to many cultures: the sunburst, repeated cresting waves, swastika, and heart.

In this way the final appearance of the stenciled wall in nineteenth century New England was just a step in the evolution of design that had developed over the centuries. Most of the patterns, the division of space, and even the terminology of the elements themselves are only variations of themes that have been used before. So don't worry about being too original. In all likelihood, you won't be.

From this it would seem that wall stenciling cannot be a creative art. This is the criticism of those who can only see its mechanical overtones. But in the hands of gifted craftsmen, strong possibilities still exist as they do in all of the decorative arts. These can be explored by anyone willing to go beyond merely adapting historical backgrounds for modern living.

In considering the elements and relationship of patterns on a wall, look at the three kinds of general arrangements that are still common today:

The Running Border These repeating lineal designs are of uniform width and—although each stencil is usually cut about 18 inches long for convenience—can be extended to indefinite length. Often, they are used to parallel the framing of doors, windows, and mantelpieces; or they are applied at regular intervals on the wall between such architectural features. The space between them is covered with a color wash but otherwise left undecorated. They may even be used to imitate some features that do not exist—such as vine-covered pilasters. Used alone, they will give the room an atmosphere of simple and restrained formality while enhancing notable aspects of the woodwork. Alone they reinforce the room's height. When used in conjunction with a more elaborate frieze at the top of the wall—one that suggests the swags and tassels of a hanging fabric, for example—the plane of the wall and the plane of the ceiling will have a

Although it is up to the discretion of the stenciler where and how to use patterns, sometimes it is also suggested by the construction. This leafy border has been used as sparingly as possible by David Wiggins.

strong visual separation. This type of layout was taken up again in the Victorian era, when stenciling experienced a rebirth.

Floating Motifs within a Panel Individual—usually alternating—motifs are stenciled within areas delineated by running vertical and horizontal border designs (which may or may not be of the same design). These borders "frame" panels. This was an arrangement frequently used by such identifiable stencilers as Moses Eaton. It is the traditional layout now commonly thought of as producing the "country" look—and the one most copied

Moses Eaton's spirit is alive and well in the backhall of an old house in New Hampshire today, but the house was only redecorated in the past three years. Note how Wiggins used his own judgment in where to float the traditional motifs: there is no pattern to their placement. The soft colors and familiar designs produce a restful room.

today. Proper placement of the motifs is the key to establishing openness. Sometimes this is done by measuring, sometimes by "eyeballing" while stenciling the motifs on the wall. The dimensions of each panel can be extended or tightened slightly without greatly disturbing the overall symmetry; thereby, the design can be made to fit what may be differing measurements of adjacent walls.

This all-over bedroom design within panels formed by running borders looks like wallpaper but was designed and stenciled by David Wiggins and his wife. Freehand brushwork complete the design.

The All-Over Pattern This is common to many wallpaper and fabric designs even today. In fabrics they are called "diaper" patterns. The same designs are repeated both vertically and horizontally. The design often includes either strongly super-imposed verticals or diagonals or both. The greatest challenge to the stenciler is planning how to fit the patterns to the dimension of the walls, for the all-over design cannot be expanded or tightened gracefully. Usually this pattern is restricted by borders that are parts of the wood framing or by other stenciled lines and borders that help frame it. Common to New England particularly, this development came later than the floating motif arrangement in the evolution of wall stenciling and, because it demands a more complicated use of stencil overlays and a wider use of color, is usually considered more sophisticated.

How to lay out and execute each of these general arrangements will be discussed more fully in Chapter 4.

Combinations of these three common arrangements are possible even within one room. One wall could be designed to carry only floating motifs within rectangular panels while the other three are stenciled with running borders and areas of negative space—the whole unified by color, a common frieze, and surbase border designs.

Or—to give a fireplace wall, for example, special treatment and an even stronger focus—individual motifs can be applied above the overmantle (a large floral bouquet, pairs of birds, the traditional weeping willows, an eagle, etc.) and the other walls stenciled with simple running borders or an all-over design. The choice is up to the decorator and the ultimate effect he or she wants to achieve.

The terminology and placement of patterns comes from conventional practices of the late eighteenth century. In this, architecture played a major part. Two of the most influential designer-builders of that period were Robert and James Adam, who rediscovered the decorative proportions and embellishments of the Roman era. In this country the architecture that they inspired and sought to copy is known as the neoclassic or federal style. Their principal find—as it relates to wall stenciling—was the classical column and its entablature, capital, shaft, dado, and pedestal. For those who could afford it, the column was incorporated into the design of some domestic architecture, either as freestanding elements or as pilasters, which are vertically segmented columns built into and projecting from the wall surface.

In this country the evolution of the Roman column can be traced from the wealthy coastal communities to the most isolated farmhouse of the early nineteenth century. For those who could not afford such built-in elegance either in wood or molded plasterwork, the divisions and proportions of the column were at least retained and refined even though the column itself was absent. These glimmerings from the past were kept for practical as well as aesthetic purposes. They can still be sensed in the baseboard and chair rail, and in the moldings that surround a colonial or modern fireplace and support the mantleshelf.

In the simplest country house of the early 1800s, heavy wooden moldings and cornices disappeared from all but the best room, wainscoating was reduced even on the fireplace wall, and the wide, single-board dado from floor to windowsill height (whose function was to provide some insulation and protection from constant wear) was replaced with plaster. However, the baseboard and chair rail were generally retained. These two architectural elements owe their origin essentially to the memory of the classical column.

The baseboard, commonly called the mopboard, is a wide board set against the bottom of the wall and usually on a plane in front of it. Sometimes it is topped by a molding that duplicates the underside of the chair rail. The baseboard corresponds to the base of the pedestal.

The chair rail—sometimes called a dado-cap even though the wooden dado between it and the baseboard has been eliminated—can be a narrow board that surrounds the room just even with the level of the windowsills. Sometimes this is set at right angles to the wall surface to form a ledge, and a molding is applied beneath it. This originally separated the pedestal of the column from its shaft.

Aside from the practical value of guarding the plaster from

SKETCH OF COLUMN OF THE ROMAN DORIC ORDER

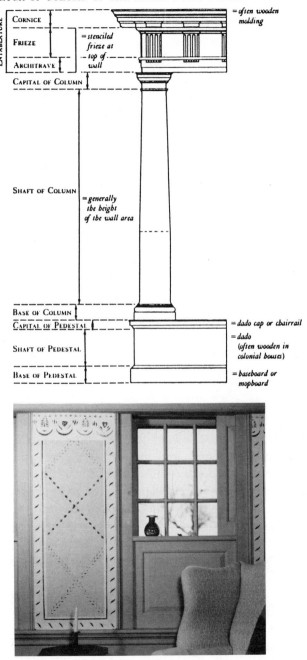

ENTABLATURE
CORNICE
FRIEZE = stenciled frieze at top of wall
ARCHITRAVE
= often wooden molding

CAPITAL OF COLUMN

SHAFT OF COLUMN = generally the height of the wall area

BASE OF COLUMN
CAPITAL OF PEDESTAL = dado cap or chairrail
SHAFT OF PEDESTAL = dado (often wooden in colonial houses)
BASE OF PEDESTAL = baseboard or mopboard

Can you recognize the architectural prototypes for these stenciled panels? Perhaps restraint is the key to achieving elegance as shown in this New Hampshire bedroom.

damage and wear, both of these elements help establish parallel, horizontal lines that contrast with the verticality of the doors and windows. Psychologically they give the occupants of the room a feeling of rest or stability—the reassurance that they are indeed fixed to the earth—which is echoed in the line of the horizon beyond the windows.

As the stenciled wall became popular, it had to take into account these structural and decorative architectural devices. And the architectural terminology has been retained to this day. Even now we speak of the *frieze*, which, in architectural design, is the central, horizontal section of the entablature between the cornice and the architrave. A stenciled frieze—usually a series of repeated patterns from four to seven inches deep—is applied under a wooden cornice or molding that arrests the eye at the top of the wall and stops it from wandering across the ceiling. If no molding is present, the frieze is often designed with reeded or fluted elements to simulate fine interior finish. The higher the ceiling and the larger the room, the deeper the frieze. In rooms with low ceilings, a deep frieze tends to dominate and therefore depress the proportions of the room as well as the rest of the design.

Often, there is also a *surbase* design. This is another running pattern, different from the frieze but frequently incorporating some of its elements, and applied just above the chair rail. If the dado is plaster rather than wood, the design sometimes appears just below the chair rail to doubly reinforce the horizontal line.

The *base border* design is applied just above the baseboard on fully plastered walls and on those which are interrupted by a chair rail. Both surbase and base border designs imitate the horizontal visual lines in the base of the column.

Vertical borders, on the other hand, simulate the shafts of the vanished column and are applied in the corner of the room where plaster walls meet and at prearranged intervals along the wall surface. Some examples actually suggest fluted columns entwined by vines; others seem content to lend height alone, for this is as necessary to human aspirations as the horizontals are to supporting a sense of stability.

A third line is also important. This is the *diagonal*. Angling

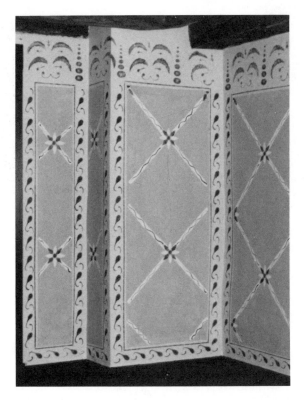

The frieze is recognizably Moses Eaton but the tinted panels, running borders, and strong, partly freehand diagonals give it away as the work of the Wigginses.

between horizontals and verticals either as running patterns or interrupted lines, diagonal can also be suggested by alternating shapes and colors to provide design interest and contrasting movement. Unless controlled, they can tip the balance between height and breadth and introduce too much confusion.

The *motifs* themselves—like those in the panel designs of Moses Eaton and even in the quarter shells sometimes inset within the corners of the panel border—probably evolved from the wooden, plastered, or painted medallions that the Adam brothers adapted from Roman design. These two-dimensional shapes add interest to the division of space and establish muted focal points. Their effectiveness in design is controlled by regular spacing, repetition and alternation, contrast and parallel-

Often less stenciling is more apt to produce the classical look—as in this 18th century bedroom where the plaster walls make a strong enough statement. They were tinted raspberry.

ism, rhythm, balance, symmetry, and proportion as well as color harmonies.

These, then, are the basic elements of wall stencil design, some or all of which were used in decorating a room in historic times and still are today. Although masked by time, their originals can be traced to ancient precedents in other art forms. Using them effectively today depends to a large degree on the size and proportions of the room you are decorating. Their shapes will also have to be scaled down to human scale for a private environment. The grandeur of the Roman temples and baths, even the high-ceilinged elegance of the neoclassic interiors, may not apply to your stenciling project. Therefore, you must base many of your design decisions today solely on personal reaction to proportions and placement of the designs.

The origins of these elements may be of only peripheral interest to today's stenciler—as they probably were to the instinctive journeyman in the early 1800s. Certainly this mechanical process of home decoration can be utilized and adapted without an extended study of historical precedents. However, even a passing knowledge of it and a familiarity with the terms will help you be more aware of some of the aspects of proportion and arrangement that are essential to all good design.

CHAPTER THREE

Consider
Design and Color

A s in any do-it-yourself home project, there will be decisions to make and materials to assemble before you can roll up your sleeves and actually begin to stencil. Once you arrive at that point, however, you will be surprised how quickly the work progresses. This chapter deals with two major areas you will have to consider on the way to that point: the overall design and color.

Of course, many of your decisions—like the choice of color and pattern, even how much or how little of each is required to achieve the best results—are purely personal. For those who already exhibit strong preferences, these choices are frequently

Stenciling this all-over pattern in five colors under a sloping ceiling would daunt the beginner. Choose simpler projects and learn as you go.

instinctive; for others, less sure, they will involve pondering various possibilities and experimenting a lot before proceding.

Begin by selecting what wall or room to stencil. Perhaps this is the easiest decision. If you are a beginner, it might be wise to choose a small entrance hall or powder room as your first challenge in using a new/old decorating technique until you have gained both experience and confidence. Still, if you already know you will limit wall stenciling to only one room in your house—despite the proficiency and enthusiasm you will surely develop—you could take on a greater challenge right away: the stairwell, dining room, bedroom, a child's nursery, or even the living room itself.

Remember that the mechanical aspects of stenciling will not vary from room to room and project to project. But each room will require a new set of measurements and present other problems: the choice and arrangement of the patterns, whether they are to be single or composite designs, what colors to use, and even what kind of paint will be most suitable for a particular room.

Inspired by the tiles in the Alhambra, Gerard Wiggins created the same Moorish effect with artifacts, two colors, and stencils.

Before you are tempted to make quick decisions, take a long, hard look at the room itself: study its size; the extent and condition of its walls; the position and distribution of its windows and doors; the condition of the woodwork; unusual architectural features like built-in cupboards, counters, chair rails, paneling; and the location of the fireplace, if any. Be aware of the direction and amount of natural light. All these will influence your decisions regarding the choice of color and pattern.

Now try to visualize the overall effect you hope to create. Do you want to make the room appear larger or smaller? Cozy or more formal? Low- or high-ceilinged? Do you want the stenciling to enhance the architecture of the room or to mask it? The mass and arrangement of the patterns will play major roles in these decisions (see pages 25 through 30). So will the judicious use of color—not just the colors chosen for the designs themselves but the color for the woodwork and the background tint you choose before you even lay a pattern on the wall.

Let's consider color. Some artists insist that manipulating

colors to get the tints you want is not much more complex than understanding black and white in which you only have values of dark and light and can move up or down the scale through a series

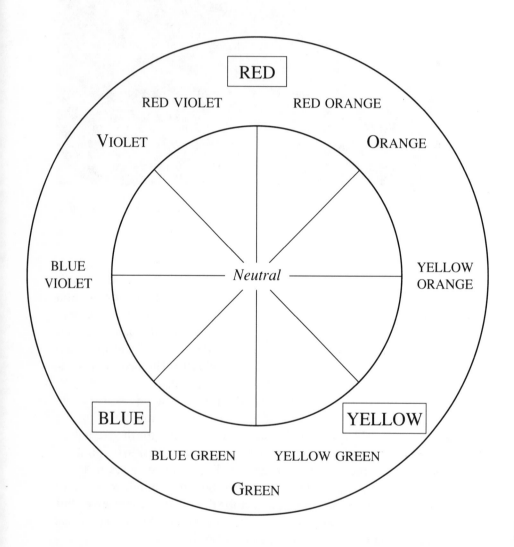

of grays. That's like playing only basic scales on the piano over and over again. The results are obviously limiting because there's not much variety. In choosing to work with color, however, you will discover a far greater range of choice. These are chromatic and tonal values that will add a whole series of harmonies to the basic scale. *Chromatric value* is the degree of intensity or purity of a color; *tonal value* is its position on a scale of light and dark. Light tones are usually referred to as tints; dark tones are called shades.

Red, yellow, and blue form the points of an isosceles triangle on the color wheel. These are the *primary* colors. By mixing any two of these primaries in varying amounts, you will discover a whole series of new hues.

For example, you can choose a can of basic red from the paint store shelf (or from a decorator color chart) that comes closest to what you think you want. Smear some of it on a piece of white paper and, when it's dry, study it in natural light. If it isn't exactly the hue you wanted, you can alter it. By adding a few drops of blue to the basic red, you can tilt toward the cool (violet) side of the wheel or, by adding yellow, toward the warm (orange) side. Follow the same procedure to alter a basic blue or a basic yellow. It is worthwhile taking the time to experiment. Then you will see the possibilities.

Lamp black, burnt umber, raw sienna, French ocher, and Prussian blue were some of the other colors that were used historically in wall stenciling. By tilting any of these colors you can come up with additional harmonies. But the first step is to study the color wheel.

When one *primary* color is mixed with another, the result is a *secondary* color (red + yellow = orange; red + blue = violet; yellow + blue = green). A primary mixed with a secondary will produce a range of other colors depending on the proportions of each (i.e., blue + green = all those varieties of hues between blue and green).

Complementary colors are those that are opposite one another on the wheel (green/red, orange/blue, yellow/violet). When used side by side, these produce strong contrast; whereas, *adjacents* (colors that fall next to — or close by — one another on the wheel)

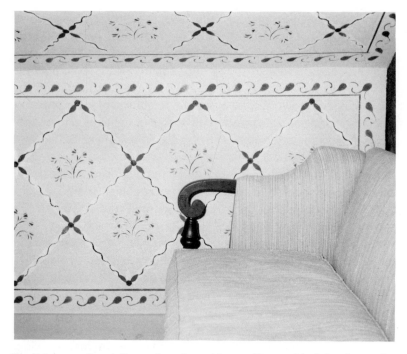

The lightly re-enforced diagonals and repetitive motifs provide design interest in this bed-sitting room under the eaves.

produce a more harmonious effect (orange/yellow, red-orange/ orange, yellow-orange/yellow, etc.).

Warm colors are those in the red to yellow segment of the wheel. Those on the red to blue side are called *cool* colors.

Used by itself, a wash of color will make a room appear larger or smaller, lighter or darker, warmer or cooler, stimulating or restful. Color can either emphasize or disguise architectural features. It can also affect our emotional outlook. Many people have an instinctive reaction to certain colors or combinations; others may respond through an associative process without knowing why. But nearly everyone reacts to color in some way.

Traditionally, certain colors were automatically chosen to decorate specific rooms because of their exposure to natural light. Interior rooms on the north—or cool—side of the house were painted with warm colors to counteract the blue reflected light from the sky and the minimal amount of direct sunlight. Those rooms facing south were decorated from the cool side of the color wheel—blues, greens, and their adjacents—to counteract or balance a naturally warm and bright environment. Today, we can legitimately thwart tradition by manipulating our surroundings with artificial light and temperature control. In this respect we are much less dependent on natural light than our ancestors were. Besides, much more is known about the psychological interaction of color and humans—and the reactions a room's color may be expected to trigger in the occupants. Therefore, colors can be used to manipulate a hoped-for reaction.

Some automatically tell us to "feel at home." We recognize the cheerfulness of yellow (associated with morning sunshine or spring flowers) and the calming effect of blues and greens (referring us subconsciously perhaps to the depth of a cloudless summer sky, the vastness of the ocean, the shadows of a late afternoon's winter landscape, or the lushness of foliage after a rain). Reds, however, stimulate our emotions by reminding us of the heat of the sun or the warmth and fascination of fire.

Our instinctive reactions to color can be used to reinforce the function of a room as well. A room intended for quiet pursuits can be reinforced by using calming colors from the cool side of the wheel. Where livelier activities take place—and more visual stimulation is required—decorators lean more heavily on warm colors to achieve a sense of drama. Cool colors will make a room appear larger; warm colors, smaller.

While the choice of specific colors or combinations is personal because it is associative and emotive, the most important aspect of color to consider in both the room and the designs is its chromatic or tonal value. Remember: *chromatic value* refers to the intensity of the color. By mixing two complements (for example, red and green) in nearly equal proportions, a gray will result. This reduces the chromatic value of both. If these are mixed in unequal amounts they will soften or neutralize one at the expense of the other (a small amount of red mixed with green softens the chromatic value of the green; a small amount of green mixed with red softens the chromatic value of the red).

Again: *tonal value* is the position of the color on a scale between light and dark. Although any two colors can be made harmonious if you limit their value, in general it is easier to harmonize adjacents. If using complements in the same stencil pattern, mix them with each other or with a common third color. For instance, in a green/red composite mix both colors with yellow to make a red-yellow and a green-yellow. Patterns using complementary color schemes usually need the addition of an adjacent color to stabilize the tension created. But the danger of using only adjacents is that the result may be an uninspiring monochrome with values too subtle to distinguish. To combat this possibility, introduce other small areas of contrast to add strength and vitality to the design. While complementary color schemes will necessarily produce strong contrast, as you neutralize them they become less blatant.

But you will soon discover that colors placed next to one another appear to behave oddly; they may seem to change in hue or intensity or depth. A blue will look different on a white wall than on a gray one. In a stencil design the same blue will appear to be slightly different when used against a red than it does when used against a green. Colors seem more intense when covering a large area. The dominant color—that which you use the most of in the largest designs—should be the most neutralized, or lightened, in tonal value. By doing this the chromatic intensity of the smaller areas will seem to increase.

Cool colors used in the same design with those from the warm segment of the color wheel will recede from the surface of the wall while warm colors advance. For example, take a design of red and blue on a white wall: the red (warm) jumps forward, the blue (cool) retreats.

The overriding impression—and much of the appeal—of an antique stenciled wall is its soft, harmonious colors where time has taken its toll and overlaid the original patterns with a patina of age, blurring the designs and making the wall a proper background rather than a focus. This effect may not have been the intention of the original stenciler more than a century ago, but since wear and exposure have made the wall look "distressed," the effects, many feel, are pleasing.

A modern stenciled wall by David Wiggins, can nevertheless recall a by-gone era. Part of the trick here is his use of adjacent colors and contrasting patterns.

Today's wall stenciler—rather than produce a finished product that looks like it was stenciled this morning—can achieve almost the same softness that elsewhere it has taken 150 years to acquire. Most of it will has to do with a considered choice of colors: how the tone and value of the woodwork matches that of the patterns, the tint that has been applied to the wall surface, the choice of adjacent hues or neutralized complements for the patterns themselves. There are also techniques for treating the wall and applying the paint that will be discussed in the following chapter.

The early stencilers used a restricted palette because they used natural pigments available to them. Some of them relied on complementary colors of high chromatic value and, where time has not been too abusive or the walls have been papered over and protected, the originals were more vivid than we expect. (Certain colors—greens and blues—have changed more than others on

Boldness of design provides the statement in this New Hampshire bedroom. The repetition of the large chainlike verticals and smaller alternating leaf patterns on a darkly tinted wall (without frieze or baseboard patterns) gives the room a surprisingly contemporary look.

the antique wall. Many appear today to be black, but black was sparsely used by the original journeymen except for occasional freehand lines or accents.) Sometimes you can glimpse what the chromatic values once were when paint was first applied to the wall. Many of the color combinations are still striking: green/red, blue/yellow, green/raspberry.

So if boldness is what you would rather have today—and you might be historically authentic—stick to colors of strong (ungrayed) chromatic value on a wash of white or off-white *and* a consistent amount of paint on your stencil brush so each design element will have crisp outlines. As before, vividness can still result today by using strong values that have not been neutralized and by selecting complementary color combinations.

Whichever way you choose to go—the muted background or the modern focus—there are two reassuring things to remember about wall stenciling: you can always overpaint whatever you have done (and will sometimes have to), and you will have discovered a lot about color, design, and yourself in the process.

CHAPTER FOUR

The Mechanics of Stenciling

When you have selected compatible colors and designs for the wall you are going to decorate, you will finally be ready to consider the mechanics of how to do it. These include cutting stencils, selecting paint, and applying colored patterns to practice boards before you actually face stenciling the wall.

Part of this can be a painstaking and messy business, particularly if the designs are intricate, several colors are to be used, or you have tried to cut too many corners before gaining insight into the problems that might arise.

Some people avoid the step of cutting stencils altogether by buying commercially prepared kits that have been machine-stamped and mass-produced. This might be easier but it limits both your freedom of choice and your innate creativity. Besides, it's more expensive.

To appreciate the entire production and retain a sense of individual freedom, you should have a direct hand in all of the decisions and operations from the beginning. This will encourage your creative spirit in many other areas.

Perfectionism should not be given too much weight in any of the following mechanical matters—although this will depend on your outlook and personality—but remember to work slowly and carefully because once they are on the wall your patterns will stand as silent testimony to your efforts. From the beginning, *aim* for accuracy because errors will seem magnified when fixed to the wall permanently, and they will be endlessly repeated wherever you use that pattern. Remember two other things also: the process should be fun, *and* you can always backpaint if a mistake or misjudgment is absolutely glaring.

THE LIMITATIONS OF STENCILING

The process of designing and cutting stencils had self-imposed restrictions. According to Robert Dossie, who wrote *The Handmaiden to the Arts* in 1764, stenciling is practical "where there are only detached masses or spots of colors; for where there are small, continued lines, or parts that run one into another, it is difficult to preserve their connection or continuity."

You cannot, for example, make a design of concentric circles with a stencil pattern. To cut one circle is, of course, possible, but as you finish cutting the outline of the second, the original circle will drop out and be lost.

The best way to illustrate the necessity of the "bridges" or "ties" that you must leave to hold the pattern together is to cite a simple example from your past. Remember how you cut snowflakes, geometric patterns, and even long lines of repeated doll shapes from folded paper as a child or parent? To re-create this now, fold a piece of paper in half and refold it several more times until it has been greatly reduced in size. With a pair of scissors cut notches, semicircles, triangles, etc., along the creased edges.

When you have finished, open up the paper and spread it on a flat surface.

Now visualize this as a possible stencil pattern. The holes through which paint could be applied are separated by "bridges." These are essential. Without them, one mass of color would be absorbed by the next and the shapes would be enlarged and changed. Therefore, these "bridges" or "ties" are necessary to plan for and leave; otherwise, the whole design would fall through and you would be left with only one large outline that is not what you had in mind.

With stenciling you will not be able to reproduce many of the lines and intricate curves that a freehand artist can. In conventionalizing the stem of a plant, for example, you will have to design it as a series of unconnected sections, especially if it is elaborate. The bridges must be broad enough to separate the masses; if too thin, paint will run under them and obliterate the precision of the pattern. When you design and cut your stencil without taking in these considerations, large sections of the pattern will literally disappear under your cutting tool.

These inherent restrictions, therefore, require that stenciling be a simple and direct method from the beginning.

TRACING A DESIGN

A more challenging method than buying prepackaged art is to find motifs you personally admire. Then duplicate them. Examples of stencil patterns are abundant once you begin to look around for them. You might take some elements from an existing wall or photograph; others from a piece of furniture such as a stenciled dresser or trunk; and more from wallpapers, lampshades, or fabrics. To copy them proceed in logical steps. You may have the ability to make a freehand drawing of what you see and then perfect it; otherwise, do a tracing and transfer this to your stencil material. If the running border or motif is a *composite* —a pattern made up of more than one color—eventually you will need to cut a separate stencil for each. However, at this stage it is easier to make just one tracing of the entire pattern, regardless of the number of colors. This will help insure that the forms will all fit together later when you separate them by color and cut individual stencils.

Either buy commercial tracing paper or, lacking this, use standard $8\frac{1}{2} \times 11$-inch typing sheets through which you can see the original design as you trace it. (If completely stuck for material, any paper can be made semitransparent by lightly coating it with cooking oil and letting it dry. If forced to use this method, remember that residual oil may leave a stain on the surface from which you are making the tracing. So make sure it is dry.)

Lay the tracing paper flat over the original pattern and center it. Make sure to leave enough margin to protect the surface and to provide space for making notes. Indicate the top of the tracing with a penciled arrow. For personal interest and your records, record the number of the tracing, the colors used in the original if you intend to duplicate them exactly, and references that will help you to recall where and when you did the tracing.

Smooth out the tracing paper with one hand as you anchor its corners with small pieces of masking tape—or better yet Easy-Mask, a paper tape used by professionals because only half its undersurface is gummy; the other is plain paper. This means both that it is easier to detach and that it will not lift off flecks of paint or plaster with its slightly sticky undersurface. Copy the outlines of the design carefully with a fine-pointed, soft lead pencil. If some of the design is blurred or the surface you are working from is particularly rough, you may have to fill in the missing parts freehand after you have taken the tracing down. Once you have completed tracing all the outlines, made your marginal notes on color, etc., remove the tape and your tracing.

You will be fortunate to find an original stenciled wall to study. From it you can trace the running border or the frieze. By looking at it closely, you will be able to see where the stenciler repeated his design. Often it will be a section about 20 inches long. Then you will see how he aligned his pattern to elongate the design. It is easier to stencil border and frieze patterns in shorter sections even though they may run 16 or more feet and completely circle a room. Once the repeat has been determined, trace the original with the same care as you would a single motif.

A modern convenience that was not available to stencilers until fairly recently will greatly simplify the job of duplicating the patterns you want to use. This is the photocopy machine. With this you can enlarge or reduce patterns with the push of a button, thereby saving yourself an enormous amount of time and effort by bypassing the arduous step of transferring the design to graph paper and calculating the adjustments by hand in order to change its proportions to fit the wall you are going to stencil.

Once you have gotten the design to fit these proportions, you will be ready to go on to the next step: actually transferring it to the stencil material.

STENCIL MATERIALS

Some early stencilers cut their designs from leather or tin. Most used whatever heavy paper came to hand. Either before or after cutting a stencil pattern they gave the paper several coats of oil, paint, or shellac to stiffen it and help make it less porous. Then it was allowed to dry thoroughly before using.

There is a wider and better range of materials to choose from today. Even a couple of decades ago one of the most common was *stencil paper*—a stiff, opaque tan or brown composition paper—which is available at art supply stores in 2 × 3-foot sheets and can easily be cut with a knife and straightedge or scissors into more manageable dimensions. A many-plied *oaktag* was sometimes used, but this tends to be less rigid and permanent for stencil making. The difficulty in using either of these materials is that they are not as pliable as others are and—in spite of applying coats of shellac to make them less porous—they are harder to clean.

Stencilers sometimes use *architect's linen*, a dully transparent, coated material that is lightweight and flexible enough to bend where bending is needed. One side is glossy, the other matte. The stenciler can cut much more delicate designs and accurate curves in this than in any paper product. But whereas the inherent flexibility is necessary for fitting a pattern to the gentle curve of a chair back or chair leg, for example, its flexibility is not particularly advantageous when stenciling the flat surface of a wall. However, the transparency is an advantage over paper in that you can see the placement of the patterns as you stencil.

Modern chemistry has come up with two products that are surely better than any of the above: *acetate* and *mylar*. The former is a plastic product, the latter a polyester. Each is semitransparent (frosty on one side, shiny on the other) and has been prepared to draw on and erase mistakes from if need be. Acetate is more brittle and it tears. At art and office supply stores they are available either in rolls or sheets and come in standard thicknesses from .003 millimeters to .0075 millimeters. Professional wall stencilers seem to prefer the thickness they are used to, but at whatever thickness, mylar is now their standard choice. Because of the dimensions available, it is particularly good for cutting and stenciling long borders, thereby avoiding having to cut the patterns up into shorter segments. And it can be easily cleaned when using oil paints by soaking them in paint thinner. Using an abrasive to clean paint from the lighter thicknesses may break up the plastic.

Cleaning the stencils after using them is essential. It prevents the buildup of layers of paint that occurred, for example, on the paper stencils of Moses Eaton. Finally, either acetate or mylar will allow you to produce sharper outlines, particularly where these come together to form points in the designs. Because of the makeup of composition paper, fine points are likely to be fibrous and fuzzy in spite of the sharpness of the cutting implement and the care of the cutter.

When pressed for stencil material—or if you have strong views about recycling—some wall stencilers use discarded x-ray film gleaned from a hospital or doctor's office. This is also an acetate and will be either transparent or semitransparent, depending on the exposure of the film, but try to come by some that is not too dark. X-ray film will lie flatter than materials that are cut from rolls but, of course, it only comes in predetermined dimensions.

Availability and cost may be the ultimate factor in choosing one kind of stencil material over another, but on today's market there is a wide selection.

TRANSFERRING A DESIGN

Now that you have either traced a design or created one of your own, determined its size, and selected your stencil material, it is time to cut it out. First, place the stencil material on a flat, even surface. If using opaque stencil paper, overlay it with a piece of carbon paper, the carbon side down. Align the tracing and tape it down. Go over the tracing with a soft lead pencil, working slowly between spread thumb and index finger.

Whereas this was a common and necessary step in the past, it is almost unheard of today. Copying machines allow you to bypass it altogether by making as many duplicate images as you need.

So if using acetate or mylar, lay either material *over* the design and don't even bother to make a tracing. Avoid this step of transferring the image by cutting your design directly. Remember this will ruin the original image but will speed the process. With simple patterns, making this sacrifice doesn't matter as much, but when you start getting interlocking or composite patterns—designs that will mean making several stencil patterns, one for each color you will use—every time you make a cut you have to be right. Therefore, it is wise to have several extra copies of the original on hand before you begin to cut your stencil because the one you need may be the one you have sacrificed and thrown away.

CUTTING A STENCIL

Now comes the exacting work. You are about to cut your design. The cutting tool you use will depend on two factors: the ease with which you can use it and the stencil material itself. Some professional stencilers use embroidery scissors with architect's linen and achieve enviable, delicate results. Wall stencilers today generally use either the single-edged razor blade or an X-acto knife. These can be purchased in hardware, hobby, or art supply stores. The X-acto knife may come with a variety of blades to choose from. It would be wise to buy several kinds—some with broad bases, others with long, tapering points—to suit different situations that may arise during the cutting process. Razor blades are expendable, but X-acto knife blades can be honed repeatedly whenever the edge show signs of dulling.

If you are using stencil paper, a single-edged razor blade will do a nice job. Exert pressure with the index finger alone on the upper edge of the blade. Even if a corner of the blade should break under pressure, you can reverse it or continue on as long as it retains a sharp point. An X-acto knife is better for architect's linen, acetate, and mylar. You will need less pressure because these materials will cut more easily. You exert this with both the index finger and thumb of your cutting hand.

Dull blades make cutting a stencil a chore. The points of your design will be the first to suffer, so make sure your blade is as sharp as possible. If using an X-acto knife, have a honing stone handy to keep the point in prime condition.

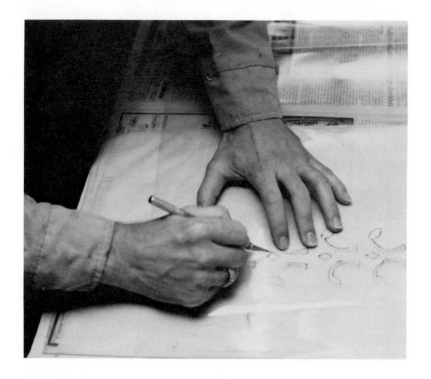

Take a piece of ordinary window glass and clear off a flat surface on which to do your cutting. Lay the stencil material on top of the glass. If glass is not available—and while dulling the blade, this hard surface will make sharper outlines possible—use many thicknesses of newspaper both to cushion material as you cut and to protect the surface below. The padding will help the point of the blade penetrate the stencil material.

Hold the X-acto knife tightly in your cutting hand at an angle of about 45 degrees, although to make deeper impressions you will have to vary this continuously from 60 to 90 degrees. Do not rest the heel of your cutting hand on the stencil itself; instead, extend your little finger slightly so that its tip will act both as a guide and a rest. To control the accuracy of the cut, particularly on curves, keep the cutting hand poised in one position while your feed the stencil away from the cutting point as you would feed fabric away from the needle of a sewing machine. This will help make long, smooth cuts.

Cut along the outside edge of the outline so the finished pattern will be the same size as the original. When each mass of the pattern has been cut, lift it out with the tip of your blade and brush it aside. You may have to trim your design later, particularly any points where the outline is not crisp. Do this by lifting the stencil from the table and shaving into the points with the center segment of the blade.

In a bygone era stencilers had to bevel the outlines of their designs because the stencils were thicker than materials available today. The beveling sharpened all the outlines while thinning the material so that when the paint was applied, it would produce crisper patterns. Using acetate or mylar, beveling is practically impossible and will not make that much difference anyway.

KEYING YOUR STENCILS

Although there is not historical precedence for this step, it's wise to take a tip from today's dress pattern manufacturers and cut a key on the edge of your stencil so you can align the different pieces of a composite stencil accurately. First make sure each has the same overall dimensions. Then lay them on top of one another and notch the edges with a successive number of Vs. These nicks do not have to be large, just enough to be able to spot and align quickly and accurately. For example, in the center of the upper edge, cut a single V; on the right, two Vs; on the bottom, three; and along the left border, four. All of these keys may not be necessary once you have gained some experience, but it is a good precaution for the beginner to take. The keys, lightly copied in pencil directly onto the wall surface, will also help you place your stencil accurately when it comes time to apply paint. Later the pencil marks should be erased.

SELECTING PAINT

Today's wall stencilers have a greater variety of paints to choose from than our predecessors did. Each type has its own virtues.

These may include the permanence of the pigment; its availability; the ease with which it can be mixed, applied, and cleaned up after; its odor; the time it takes to dry; and its cost.

Some paints also have distinct drawbacks you should weigh before making your choice: milk paint will always dry flat and can never be cleaned; acrylic paints dry too quickly and therefore cannot be worked over; latex paints, whether in a shiny or flat finish, produce a dead "plastic" look; oil paints may bother those with allergic reactions or those who are environmentally conscientious.

Paint is made by suspending pigment—particles of color—in a medium until a hard coating develops to protect it from the effects of the atmosphere. The enduring quality of the paint and its ability to withstand cleaning may be major considerations in your choice. For example, wall stenciling in rooms of high humidity and wide temperature fluctuations—like a bathroom or kitchen—will demand a permanent paint that can be periodically scrubbed. A wall that is likely to receive continuously hard wear, such as a stairwell, must also face cleaning without disfiguring your decoration. However, walls away from the heaviest wear and tear of daily life could lead you to make a different selection.

Milk Paint

Milk paint was common in early times because both dry pigments and milk were easily available. The former could be bought from the general store or discovered and refined from natural deposits that are still abundant in New England. Milk, in a rural society, was a common commodity. Dry pigments were easy to transport and could be mixed in varying batches as needed as long as milk had been set out to sour. Then the homesteader mixed lime, whiting, pigment, and sour milk to produce a flat paint that was common, inexpensive, and universally accepted. Its disadvantages were that it was messy to mix and time-consuming to match a supply that was already depleted; it dries flat; and it is water soluble and therefore cannot be cleaned.

It was universally used as a color wash on unprimed early pine or oak furniture because it would soak into the grain of the wood but leave enough pigment to dispel the raw look. It is still used today for this purpose, for it gives unfinished furniture a veneer of instant age.

As far as the nineteenth century wall stenciler was concerned, milk paint was applied as a color wash to a plaster wall that had been lightly primed. A wash (as in *whitewashing*) is a happenstance way of laying color on a wall to allow the inconsistencies—lights and darks, the unevenness of the plaster—to show. This was done with a wide brush or a rag. When the wash dries, you can see the brush marks and the drips.

Milk paint was rarely used historically as the paint choice for stenciling the designs themselves because these, when cleaned, would vanish. For patterns the stenciler used oil-based paint but often over a light milk-paint wash.

However, the home manufacture of milk paint today—provided you can ferret out the ingredients—can be an engrossing part of any stenciling project and, in its limited way, will be both historically accurate and useful. It will not only duplicate a process used by the early stencilers, but will also lend a certain aura of tradition and produce a natural glow to the wall, as well as prove that the hand of man had something to do with the results.

So if you are a purist and want to make a milk-paint wash—but cannot find a source for milk paint today—use the following recipe:

1. Sour 2 cups (16 ounces) milk by adding 1 to 2 tablespoons of vinegar and warming it slightly on the stove until it forms curds.
2. Add ½ ounce slaked lime to the curds and whey. This will cause a chemical reaction to set in. Check with litmus paper for a neutral balance between acidity and alkalinity. When the neutral condition is achieved—and you may have to use several pieces of litmus paper before this occurs—the color of the paper will not change. It will just look wet.
3. Separate some of this mixture and set aside a portion to use later.
4. Now mix in 20 ounces whiting to form a paste. If too

thick to work, add a little of the mixture that you have reserved.

5. Add dry paint pigment by the spoonful to the paste and stir until the desired hue is achieved. It is better to add too little than too much at a time. More can always be added later.

6. Aim for a working consistency of cream. This can be made more liquid by adding more of the milk/lime mixture.

If you decide not to go that historical route, you can make an equally effective color wash with oil paints and less fuss. Besides, this will be washable. For this recipe you will need: one part of the color you have chosen for a tint, one part paint thinner, one part Penatrol, and one part of liquid glaze. This is the mixture used by decorators for graining, marbling, and faux work as well as by today's professional wall stencilers.

Paint thinner extends oil paint but, by using this alone, you will not be able to control the wash. It will run down the wall. Penatrol is the commercial name of a linseed-oil product that is used to extend an oil-based paint also. It is sold in paint stores and some hardware stores. Liquid glaze is sold by nationwide paint companies—by Benjamin Moore Paint Company, for example, as Transparent Glazing and Blending Liquid, and by Johnson's Paint Company, Newbury Street, Boston, under its own label. This makes oil paint more transparent.

When you have mixed these four components, take a natural-bristle brush about six inches wide and put it on the wall in a cross-hatch motion. Try not to cover but to wash the wall with a thin, transparent coating on which to lay out your designs. If you want it really thin, use a rag; if thicker, lay on two or three coats. This is what old-timers called "glazing a wall." One thin coat is called a wash; two or three, a glaze. Modern decorators have been known to apply eight to ten coats of this solution (often changing tints as they apply successive layers) until the wall takes on a deep, almost leatherlike appearance. With this method painters can even make sheetrock look like plaster walls.

Oil Paint

Oil paints have been used for centuries by fine artists and for generations by house painters. It is still the popular choice of the professionals. Oils can be purchased in tubes or jars at art supply stores or in larger volumes at a paint or hardware store. Oils are relatively expensive compared to other kinds of paint and have been losing their appeal in the face of rising environmental concerns, because some of the ingredients in the extenders are toxic. Their greatest attribute is that the colors will be as permanent as you can find. Another is that they are easy to make corrections with before they dry and, once dry, they will stand up to repeated cleanings. Professionals believe that in the treatment of old wood in particular, oils do a better job of preservation than some more modern paints. Whereas they are often messy to clean up after and traditionally retain their odor until dry, modern science has made some welcome modifications.

For those who have allergic reactions, oil paint companies are now manufacturing odorless paints that have an alkaline resin rather than oil base. It would pay to inquire about these since wall stenciling is a project that will probably be done when windows and doors are closed.

For those concerned with the effect of dumping toxic wastes in our environment, there are two avenues to consider and explore. For the most part it is not the oils but the thinners that are more toxic. Used paint thinners, if left standing, will separate. The liquid may be reused and the sludge saved for the next hazardous waste cleanup day.

A paint that smells like citrus and is based on natural oils is being distributed in this country by a German paint manufacturer under the brand name of Livos (see page 117, Notes on Supplies). It was developed during the mid-1970s when environmental laws were tightening up and, although likely to be expensive, would be a good product to look into. It works and acts and behaves like an oil-based paint, but it uses all-natural ingredients and is biodegradable. It is being targeted for the professional decorator/painter trade.

Japan Paints

Japan oil paints are available in either tubes or cans at a paint or art supply store. You can mix your own colors. Because the pigments are ground in a quick-drying varnish, they have the double advantage of speed drying and permanence of color. Professional wall stencilers find wet mistakes and misjudgments can be easily erased by rubbing them out with paint thinner on a rag and then proceeding immediately with the correction. When Japan paints are used by tray stencilers, they are protected by layers of clear varnish; when used for wall stenciling, they are left exposed to create a flat finish.

Latex Paint

The best alternative to using oil paints is latex. It replaced caseins, which are no longer manufactured, and these in turn evolved from the traditional milk paints. Commercial manufacturers today sell more latex paints than oils for several reasons: they are water soluble, permanent, relatively odorless while being applied, and less expensive. Besides, for those who don't mix their own colors, there is a wide range of "decorator colors" available to choose from. Although not as quick drying as acrylics, latex will firm up quickly enough to stencil fairly rapidly without the danger of smearing. Once dry the colors are permanent and can be washed. Cleanup and conditioning of the brushes can be done with soap and water. The consistency of the paint can be controlled by adding a small amount of water to make it more runny or exposing it to the air to make it more stiff.

On the other hand, professionals vastly prefer using oil paints. For one thing, oils add more depth and complexity to the wall surface. For another, being slower drying, oils can be "worked" by decorators who do graining and marbling. Latex cannot be. One stenciler suggests that if you're satisfied with sheetrock and rollers, you'll be satisfied with latex paints; if you want a more solid look and results that show they have been touched by a human hand, plaster and oil paints are the answer. This could be translated to mean "beauty is in the eye of the beholder."

Acrylic Artist Paints

Acrylics are a relatively recent development of the plastics industry. They are extremely fast drying and permanent. Purchased at an art supply store, the basic colors can be mixed together and with water to establish the proper consistency. Errors can be corrected with a damp cloth immediately, but once the paint has dried it is there permanently (but can be painted over). Professionals say acrylics dry too quickly, are somewhat rubbery to apply, and make it hard to clean the stencils. Acrylics are an option—particularly if you're interested in speed and are by nature precise. But they limit your creative freedom.

The characteristics of one of these types of paint will surely match your working habits and the degree of commitment you can make to your project in both time and money. Since cost is also a factor, you should remember the amount of paint needed to stencil a room will be very small. Therefore, don't buy large amounts of paint unless you can use the excess.

CHOOSING AN APPLICATOR

There are several ways to apply paint through the stencil cutouts. The traditional method is tapping—rather than stroking—on the paint with a blunt-ended or slightly rounded stencil brush. Another is by using a small square of fabric wrapped around the index finger. Some stencilers use artists' brushes; a few use rollers (especially when stenciling floors). Each method should be considered because slightly different effects can be produced depending on how you manipulate the applicator. That is where practice boards come in.

A contemporary method of applying patterns should be mentioned and then quickly dismissed: the spray-can approach. It is often hazardous to use indoors, the colors must be accepted as they come from the can, and the results are both uniformly dull and hard to control. Still, it is being touted by some modern decorators. If "fogging" the patterns is its principle asset, the same effects can be achieved with a stencil brush and a stenciler willing to experiment.

Early stencilers used big-headed brushes, as do most professionals today. These are wooden-handled applicators that come in various lengths and diameters. The stiff bristles are squared off or slightly rounded rather than angled or tapered. The full diameter of the brush can make contact with the stencil and the wall beneath it, but different effects can be achieved by holding the brush at various angles and by limiting the amount of paint.

PRACTICE BOARDS

Practice boards are essential aids for the wall stenciling process. It is on these that you will do most of your planning so that when everything has been tested, decorating the room will go quickly and smoothly. On these you can check the effects of the design, the alignment of parts of a composite stencil, and the compatibility of the elements. They are necessary as palettes to test color intensity, color harmony, and the changes that occur when one color is laid out adjacent to another. And using a practice board will test and develop your technique.

Many early stencil patterns have been found laid out on the end walls of an attic or in the depths of a closet where the journeyman apparently demonstrated the range of his designs and colors to the homeowner before a final judgment could be made. Rather than use a blank wall on which to experiment—and later paint out—find some portable practice boards. These might be large pieces of heavy cardboard, wood, wallboard, sheetrock, etc. Give them a primer and a coat of tinted wash and let dry. If adjustments are needed in design or color, it will be easier to paint them out on the practice board than to redo an entire section of wall. To help form your judgment, you can move the boards to different places in the room you are decorating. This will help test the effect under different light conditions.

Using practice boards will also help you perfect stenciling techniques and effects long before you begin the real job. The added confidence you gain will make the whole project run smoothly—as though this were the kind of thing you'd been doing for a long time.

USING THE APPLICATOR

Here are some tips on technique to keep in mind as you stencil.

Tape or hold the stencil flat against the wall. If the stencil moves, it will cause distortions and paint smears, so spread the fingers of one hand on each side of the cutout as you apply paint with the other. Use Easy-Mask tape rather than masking tape, for it will be easier to detach and will not lift paint with it as you pull it off.

The consistency of the paint is important. It should be neither too liquid (which would cause the paint to run under the

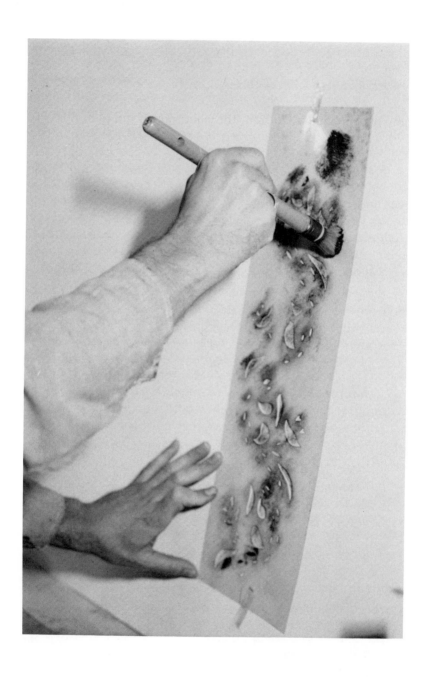

stencil) nor too thick (which makes it hard to apply where you want it).

It's better to have too little paint on the applicator than too much. One way to gauge the right amount is to have a pile of newspapers handy. Go from the paint pot to the pile. Soak up excess paint by tapping the brush into the newspapers until the paint is coming off the bristles with a fog or spraylike effect.

Feather the paint into the stencil cutout. Start applying paint at the edges of the cutout (to make these outlines crisp) and work toward the center. As the brush runs out of paint, the centers will become less covered or solid. This is the stipling effect of antique stenciling. Don't be afraid of leaving gaps where there is no paint. Otherwise, your patterns will stand out starkly from the wall. The openness of the results will depend both on the design and your technique. Stipling is a time-honored technique. To get an even more "distressed" look, modern stencilers 1) make sure brush marks are left visible in the wash, 2) sometimes sand areas of the wall to expose or roughen more of the plaster and allow it to show through the wash, and 3) work to get the mottled effect both by stipling as they stencil and by applying only the slightest amount of paint to some parts of the design or skipping some parts altogether. These are all ways of giving a new wall the appearance of instant age. Another method is to vary the shade of the color in any given area. For example, in a leaf pattern, apply a light shade of green, allow it to dry, and over-stencil it with a darker shade of green.

Work from the top to the bottom of each design. This will lessen the danger of crossing wet areas and smearing your patterns. When you've finished applying the first color of a composite design, put down the applicator and release the stencil. Pull it out and away from the wall. Be sure the paint is completely dry before you align your second stencil on top of it.

Keep your stencils clean. Paint builds up. It may cause smearing, if wet, or lumps under the stencil, if caked. As solvents use turpentine or paint thinner for oils and Japan paints; water for milk paint, acrylics, and latex. The paint buildup on the underside is the most insidious. Caked paint can also change the shapes of the design by reducing the size of the cutouts—

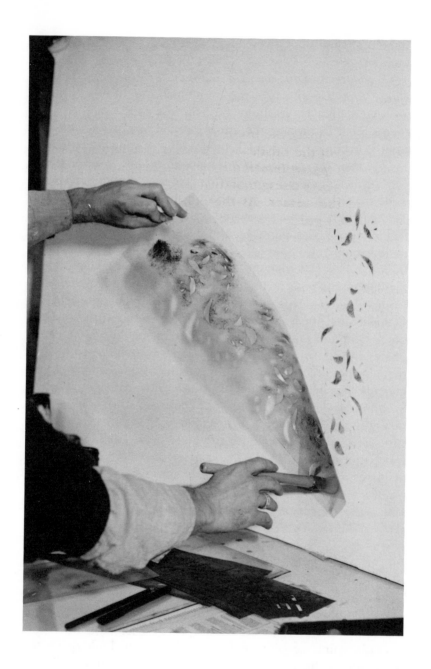

particularly in acutely angled points or in patterns that consist of many fine lines. After you clean the stencil take the tip of the X-acto knife and scrape away any excess paint that is still clogging the points of the design.

Store stencils flat when not in use. Lay these down on newspapers when dry, then cover and weight them down so they will be in good, clean condition when you are ready to resume work.

Inevitably, despite all the care and attention you give your work, some mistakes and misjudgments seem bound to occur. These may vary from slight smudges and runs to an inconsistent color if you have mixed color in too-small batches. Sometimes, it may be a major displacement of a design. Whether or not to correct these will depend on how bad you think the error is (remembering also that you will be far more conscious of it than the casual observer); how to correct it will depend on the type of paint you are using and if it is still wet when you catch the mistake. Either leave it alone or take steps to make it right.

If the paint is still wet, dip a piece of cloth in the appropriate solvent, rub out the error, let the wall dry, and stencil it again. If dry, minor mistakes and spills can be corrected by using a small artists' brush and some of the background paint to paint out the mistake. Otherwise—particularly to redeem large blunders (like stenciling one motif when you'd intended to reach for another)— overpaint the whole section of wall. Let it dry thoroughly and begin again. Relax. It's not the end of the world.

CHAPTER FIVE

Laying Out a Wall

Becauseeach room will call for flexibility of approach to laying out patterns on a wall—and some will contain their own obvious solutions—only general observations and the experience of others can be suggested here.

Remember in Chapter 2 it was stated that there are basically only three kinds of layouts—or variations of them—that will concern you in wall stenciling: running borders, floating motifs within a panel, and the all-over design. Presumably by now you have decided which of these is going to be right for you, the room you are stenciling, and the effect you want to create.

All stencils should be cut with wide enough margins so that

ABOVE AND ON FOLLOWING PAGE A frieze and vertical borders are all that is needed to give this entrance hall a touch of quiet elegance. Note how both re-enforce the architectural elements.

when you apply paint to the wall none of it will appear where you do not want it. On all the running patterns, these margins should also be a consistent distance from the cutouts themselves and have square edges. When held or taped against the ceiling, corners, or framing, this stencil margin will automatically give you a true line that you can take advantage of and thereby avoid additional measuring and marking on the wall.

Gerard Wiggins insists there is no formula, and yet, for the most part, he approaches wall stenciling in a more methodical way than his brother. They agree it's a matter of personalities. David Wiggins relies more on instinct. Often he "eyeballs" spatial relations and moves designs around until he's satisfied they *feel* right. Essentially at some stage Gerard does this too—particularly where he wants a "country" look—but both have years of experience behind them. And both admit that it's easy to make mistakes. However, neither is afraid of overpainting or backpainting a project and beginning again when that's the only thing to do.

David Wiggins admits he sometimes can't decide whether or not an all-over design should take a frieze with so much design going on until after he's nearly finished the wall. But he knows he can always band one in later if he finds it's a necessary element.

Look at the condition of your walls first. Do any necessary repairing, plugging of holes, and sanding before you give it a primer coat (if a new wall) and a tinted wash. Then apply a finish coat of paint to all the woodwork. Finally you will be ready to stencil.

One way to approach stenciling it is to take measurements of all the walls and make elevation drawings so that on paper at least you will know where to place the patterns. This is the truly methodical approach. If it's your way, your sketch should show each wall area, the distances from floor to ceiling, the distance between architectural features such as corners, window and door frames, fireplace, chair rail, etc. All of this is not really necessary, of course, but if it makes you feel more comfortable using this approach, by all means do it.

You should have the following aids at hand:
—a metal tape measure
—a carpenter's level, drop line, or chalk line
—soft lead pencils and erasers
If you are decorating an oddly shaped room or one that has settled with age, you might achieve better results by not trying

These two running border patterns frame a panel of negative space. The corners are accented by simple medallions.

for absolute accuracy. Otherwise, where only a few angles are true, your designs could be at odds with already established visual lines. With a practiced eye some stencilers can adjust spaces as they work so these correspond to structural variations. Most at least try to get vertical lines plumb.

The Running Border These are the simplest patterns to

Stencil decoration enhances the formality of this New Hampshire dining room because it is restrained both in color and pattern.

apply, whether single or composite, because they are adjacent to something: the ceiling, the woodwork (window and door frames, mopboard, chair rails, etc.), and run down the wall at each corner of the room. If there is no chair rail, decide whether or not you need a horizontal running border to carry out the design and give it added stability. Traditionally this would be on a line with the windowsills. If you decide to omit it, the wall will appear to be higher. Are you going to drop the vertical design on each side of the window frames down to the mopboard and leave it at that? Or will you use it—or another border pattern—horizontally under the windowsill? Without a frieze you could also frame in the tops of the windows and doors with design. There are a lot of possibilities even using only running borders.

But if a frieze is part of your design, start at the top of the wall and lay that out first—beginning at one corner of the room at ceiling height and stenciling around all four walls with one color. By the time you have done this the paint will be dry and—for a composite design—you can complete the frieze with a second color and then a third.

Decide, however, if it matters to you where the vertical borders are going to meet the frieze elements. For most stencilers this junction is not important, particularly if the elements in the frieze are small or fine. But if it matters to you, you better do some measuring and marking first. And if the frieze is the kind you can space out or contract slightly, now is the time to do it in anticipation of the next step: dropping the vertical designs.

With the frieze and minimum verticals applied, now decide if you want more verticals than those in the corners and alongside the windows and doors. If so, measure the distance between already applied patterns, establish equal distances, pencil mark them, and make sure your projected additions will be plumb before proceeding.

Floating Motifs within a Panel This one is a little more complicated to lay out but not much if you approach it step by step. Ideally the panels formed by your vertical borders should be of equal dimensions. It is possible to achieve this symmetry on each wall by doing some measuring and marking first, taking into account also the elements in the frieze. The trick comes when

Although this mosaic pattern for a child's bedroom shows its Moorish influence, the stenciler has combined the three general pattern arrangements: the running border, the all-over design, and the panel conception.

you find the room is not altogether square. This means panel width will vary from one wall to the next. If this is the case, the easiest thing is to tackle one wall at a time and each as a separate unit, making any adjustments in the width of the panels either by measuring or eyeballing. Forget about the floating motifs until after the frieze, surbase, and verticals have all been stenciled. Most stencilers at least complete the frieze all the way around the room first. Then drop the verticals.

The motifs that give the classic country look associated with Moses Eaton are generally about 13 vertical inches apart from center to center. So find and mark the center vertical line of each panel and along this line mark where the centers of the motifs will lie. Or tape the motif cutouts along the line and stand back to study their spacing. If you have started measuring from the top of the panel and the motif at the bottom looks crowded (or you end up with only part of it), this is where you'll obviously have to make some readjustments.

Some professionals insist that exact placement doesn't matter. Where the motif lands, it lands, they say. Slight eccentricities give it that hand-painted look and a little character. It's not like you have to put it all down on graph paper to get pleasing results. Probably the way you approach the spacing—or wall stenciling in general—is a manifestation of your own personality. After all, ultimately you are the one to satisfy first.

The All-Over Design This is the one that will most closely resemble wallpaper and the one that is the most difficult to stretch or contract. Forethought and measuring are essential before stenciling if you are copying someone else's design, because you will have to figure out on the spot how to make it fit seamlessly. This can be difficult, for example, if you come to a corner and find you only have room for a portion of a design. In that case, to get around the corner and start on the next wall, you will have to bend your stencil and make it fit (a difficult maneuver at best) or sacrifice the stencil, tape the usable part against the corner, stencil the pattern and cut another before you can proceed.

If you are creating your own all-over design, of course, you have an advantage because you've taken all the necessary mea-

These vertical running patterns could have been imprinted on wallpaper. Instead, they were stenciled on a washed plaster wall that still shows the artist's brushwork.

surements before you go to the drawing board and the stencils you cut will fit the dimensions of your room.

To avoid the look of what some might call a poor job of overall spacing—when it's too obvious, for example, there's a break in the patterns or an unfortunate seam that should have been overcome—you could surround your all-over designs with obvious stenciled margins which would be easier to juggle than the crowded patterns themselves. In this case, wash a tint on the wall in the area that will become a panel and, when this has dried, use Easy-Mask to establish the margins and tint these rectangular strips a different color. In other words, make it obvious that you are establishing the dimensions of the all-over design. It will be easier to expand or contract these marginal borders than the all-over patterns and you will have avoided a booby trap of sorts.

If, however, you opt for only an all-over design and no marginal running borders to limit it, you're going to have to recut some stencils if you get into a tight spot. Remember if you bisect a pattern accurately, you can always salvage the other part and use it, too, or you can take an artists' brush and do some freehand work to complete the designs.

But you have to start somewhere. With the all-over design more time should be spent in measuring and settling on possibilities. When you study the pictures of different all-over patterns included in this book, in some cases you will see the stenciler cut off his designs where they meet a corner—ironically just the way you would if you were wallpapering and not stenciling. So there are practical and artistic solutions to any problem if this is the kind of design you have decided on.

Wall stenciling and designing are flexible arts. What you stencil on your walls need not be traditional patterns or even ones that are suggestively derivative. You can copy something that appeals to you or you can create designs that are all your own.

APPENDIX A

Painted
and Stenciled Floors

THE TRADITION OF PATTERNED FLOORS

The New England custom of decorating wooden floors with geometric shapes and bold color was another manifestation of Yankee ingenuity that used inexpensive materials to re-create popular fashions.

Actually, the tradition of patterned floor treatment goes further back in history than wall stenciling by several thousand years. From ancient times geometric floor designs were executed in public buildings and houses of the wealthy in marble, mosaic, quarry, and ceramic tile. Later, in northern Europe, hardwood parquet floors became popular where floor warmth was a major

Bold pattern of alternating squares greets the visitor to this New Hampshire farmhouse. Scribing the floor helps contain the colors.

consideration and imported marble expensive. It was the inventive Yankee of the late eighteenth century, however—whose practiced eye was attuned to economy and an eager market—who used different colors on native pine floorboards to simulate the fashions of the wealthy. By the nineteenth century the American artisan found he could do a job more quickly and offer a wider variety by using stencils to pattern the floor.

As with the stenciled wall—which appeared later in this country than painted floors—the tradition of patterned floors bowed to later progress. Cheaper wallpapers replaced the stenciling, and painted canvas floor covers were substituted for paint on the floor until manufactured carpets came within economic reach of the homemaker sometime in the middle of the nineteenth century.

Unless they were covered over by a later fashion, not many original patterned floors from the late eighteenth century remain to be seen today, for they were subject to constant wear and, if not periodically retouched, eventually disappeared altogether. Painted floor decoration first appeared in the late 1700s. Evidence of the tradition of decorating floors in a variety of ways (freehand designs, painting overall geometric shapes, or stenciling) can be gleaned from many early American portraits of this period. It is debatable whether all the floors thus depicted in portraiture were actually a part of the interior decoration or whether they were merely flights of fancy on the part of the artist that might make his wares more salable. Art historians have taken both sides. However, as a part of the interior many bold patterns can be discerned under the feet of the sitters.

Before painted floors appeared, designs were often traced in sand that had been brought into the house to scour and sanitize the wooden floors. These were impermanent decorations that were executed with a broom or a turkey wing—perhaps the same one used to sweep the hearth and brick bake oven. The custom may have been invented to occupy active children and inspire them to be creative or merely to give special treatment to the best room in the house. However attractive it was (and the custom apparently lasted well into the last century in rural homes), pat-

Squares, rectangles, and diamonds were laid out on random width floorboards and then marbleized to make the floor seem what it is not. Only the joints give away the illusion.

terns traced in sand were transient. Painting designs on the floor was a more permanent device.

Squares, diamonds, and cubes were the most popular geometric shapes used to decorate floors and the easiest to lay out and paint if one did not have a bent for freehand decoration. Later, for a brief time, stenciling on wooden floors made an appearance, and after the 1840s the custom of splatter painting on a uniform ground gained wide acceptance. Its popularity was perhaps due to its total lack of pattern or to its greater ability to mask spills than was possible in large areas of pattern.

At the beginning of the trend in floor decoration, most attempts were made to copy the black-and-white marble checkerboard designs of the European great houses. These contributed a degree of graciousness and opulence to an entry hall or enlarged the perspective of a formal room by drawing the eye back into space. They were also a standard design that could be used with all types of furnishings.

Paint being a more flexible medium than stone, some designers introduced more variety of shapes than the endlessly repeated alternating squares or diamonds of the checkerboard pattern. One of these—the building-block design—had been done in mosaic on the Greek island of Delos more than three thousand years ago. Translated into the medium of paint, this pattern creates an optical—and often confusing—illusion. The longer you look at it, the more depth it seems to take on. Viewed from different angles, the intersecting lines and opposing blocks of color can disconcert the viewer's equilibrium. For those with weakening eyesight, this type of patterned floor may create more problems than it attempts to solve. However, the strength of the pattern—depending on the size of the painted areas and on their color—can be made to mask irregularities in floor construction or to simulate boards of different widths than have actually been used.

Whether painted on the floor by a journeyman or by the homemaker, all of these designs required only pots of paint, brushes, a measuring stick, and a little ingenuity. If patterned floors are applied today, they can be made more permanent than in the past with the application of several coats of commercial sealer and then, from time to time, wax.

Stenciling patterns on the floor—having first painted it a uniform ground—takes some planning to place the design accurately, but the techniques of doing either a wall or a floor are the same. The design can be repeated quickly and accurately merely by applying paints through the cutouts and letting them dry before they are sealed.

As with wall stenciling, the patterned floor—especially in the best room or entrance hall—was another attempt to follow fashion that began in the late 1700s and ended in the mid-1900s. It was another way of bringing color, design, and economy into the New England household.

THE TECHNIQUE OF PAINTING FLOORS

If you have ever had a nightmare about painting yourself into a corner with no escape until the paint dries, imagine how confusing it would be using different-colored patterns, none of which fit the size of your foot. This could happen to you unless you do some accurate planning—which includes scheduling time for the room to be free until the paint dries. In spite of the inconvenience, patterns painted on wooden floors are visually stimulating and well worth the effort.

Although any kind of paint can be used on wooden floors, the most permanent will be commercial deck or floor paint— either flat or glossy—that can be sealed later with several coats of polyurethane or paste wax or both. Aside from the paints, the materials you will need are brushes (their size and number determined by the kind of pattern and how many colors you plan to use), a metal measuring tape or wooden yardstick, a roll of Easy-Mask, and pencils. If planning a checkerboard or building-block pattern and you intend to scribe the design on the floorboards as the colonials did, you will also want a double-edged chisel and a hammer. To mark out long, straight lines a chalk line is also a handy accessory.

For a stenciled floor you will, of course, cut your designs in stencil material as you would for a stenciled wall, and you should have either one or more stencil brushes handy or—to do a quicker job—be prepared to apply your designs with a paint roller. Most of the professionals today choose the latter method.

PREPARING THE FLOOR

The best time to paint a floor is to pick a clear, dry day and empty the room as completely as possible. Scrape off any loose paint that may have flaked, make what repairs are necessary, and give it a good cleaning. Make sure it has completely dried before applying any paint at all; otherwise, it may peel off after you have finished. Only if you are planning a stenciled floor will you need to give the boards two coats of background color. For straight geometric designs each shape should be painted twice anyway. This can be done either over the previous coats of paint or on raw new boards.

Subdued colors and compatible tonality would give this entrance hall the patina of age even if the house were not several centuries old.

THE CHECKERBOARD DESIGN

The common shapes for checkerboard designs are squares or diamonds, although these can be arranged with other geometric masses to make pleasing patterns. If your color scheme calls for black-and-white alternating shapes, use an off-white and a grayed black. This combination will show less dirt and not assume too stark a look after it is finished.

First determine the size of the squares. Next, you will want to orient them to the room so that diagonal lines will lead the eye where you want the feet to follow. This can be done by studying the floor area from different vantage points. Diamond shapes will elongate the perspective; squares will tend to compact the room.

Once you have determined the perspective, you will have to decide how far the pattern is to be carried out. Usually, the checkerboard design is taken to the baseboards along each wall and the pattern ends there in a series of half-diamonds or half-squares. However, you could consider painting a solid color border around the perimeter of the room and placing your design centered within it as if you had laid down a patterned carpet. Whichever you decide, you will have to take notes on the dimension of the area and plan the placement of the design if it is going to come out evenly.

Common measurements for the squares of the alternating pattern are from 12 to 16 inches, depending on the size of the room to be decorated. Diamonds can be 19½ x 17½ inches from point to opposing point with four 13-inch sides, as they are in a restored room at the New Hampshire Historical Society in Concord.

Measure the area of the floor. On scratch paper determine what size the shapes must be to fit your dimensions. If this cannot be done in theory, use graph paper to plot the placement. Then transfer this to the floor. Another way is to cut out several similar blocks of diamonds from paper or cardboard and lay them on the floor, working them across the room to check whether or not they will come out evenly and where you want them.

Now use a measuring tape and chalk line to lay out the pattern accurately. For example, to lay out 12-inch squares, snap parallel chalk lines a foot apart all across the room. Snap a second series of parallel chalk lines that cross the first set at right angles.

Scribing the floorboards—or lightly incising lines in the floor with a doubled-edged chisel—was a method practiced by some journeymen of earlier times. This makes painting in the geometric shapes easier, for the lines will prevent paint from spilling over into another area when you are applying each color. It will also help assure straight lines. If you do not prefer this method because you wonder if you might change your mind about the pattern several years down the road, use long pieces of Easy-Mask to set out the pattern. This will serve much the same purpose but will mean pulling up and resetting the tape many times as you work your way across the room.

You can either paint the floor using two colors and two brushes alternately or start in one corner of the room and work your way toward a door with one color only. The former method will allow you to finish the whole project in one operation and then leave it alone until time for a second coat. If the room can be completely cut off from traffic, this method would be preferable. If it can't be, you will have to do a balancing act to paint in the second color once—and then twice over to put on the second coat of each color.

After the second coat is dry, use the floor for several weeks. This will wear away its newness slightly and give it a little character. Then clean the floor and seal it with two coats of polyurethane.

Building-Block Design

This is a more difficult pattern to lay out and a more tedious one to paint. It is composed of squares and rhomboids—geometric figures whose angles are oblique and adjacent sides unequal—to give it its three-dimensional illusion on a flat surface. It is usually painted in three colors; sometimes one of the rhomboids is over-striped or over-stenciled with a fourth.

Lay out parallel lines with a chalk line or measuring tape from one side of the room to the other. Using the same measurement, run a second series of lines at right angles to the first, thus

An optical illusion has been created in this painted combination of squares, diamonds, and rhomboids. Note the striping that softens the austerity.

forming a uniform grid. Now run a third set of lines that will bisect the squares on the diagonal in one direction only. You cannot scribe this pattern onto the floor because the incisions would overrun many of the shapes you want to paint. Instead, use short pieces of Easy-Mask to contain the colors in the patterns as you paint. Unless you can leave a great deal of time for the paint to dry before going on to another color, it's better to use the color alternatively and concurrently. This may be a confusing process at first but will begin to make sense once you see the colored patterns emerging. But don't blink. It's easy to apply paint in the wrong place if you lose your concentration. Since these shapes are generally smaller than the areas in a checkerboard design, use smaller brushes so you can negotiate accurate lines. When the floor is completely dry after the second coat, seal it as you would the checkerboard design.

STENCILED FLOORS

A faster method of painting a pattern on a floor, of course, is to stencil it. And you can do it even faster if you use a paint roller. After you have prepared the floor and given it a cleaning, you must apply two coats of deck paint before beginning to lay on the design. While it is drying you can be cutting out your patterns.

Acetate or mylar have clear advantages over other kinds of stencil materials because you can see through them. This will help in placing continuous patterns on the floor. Although these materials could curl when used on a wall unless taped down securely, they are easier to use on a floor: just anchor down the near corners with your knees, thus freeing one hand to pin down the far side while you use the other to apply the paint. With either a roller or a brush, work from far to near. Then lift your stencil, backtrack, and stencil the cutouts again.

All sorts of stencil designs can be adapted for use on the floor. Unless you plan a symmetrical repeated border around the perimeter of the room, however, none of the motifs should have a recognizable top or bottom, because this would limit the design when viewed from different angles in the room. Within

This stenciled floor in the guest room of a Vermont farmhouse looks as if a carpet has been laid down on the pine floor. The darker boarder with its right-angle lines has been carried around the perimeter of the room by the stenciler, David Wiggins.

the border design this would not be a major consideration; presumably the top of the design there would point toward the baseboard and the bottom out into the room.

Another factor may be decided on the basis of personal judgment alone: whether the designs should be bold and stark or intricate and subtle. This may be determined by the function of the room or how the rest of it is decorated.

The easiest stenciled floor design to apply is either an allover pattern of one design or one of alternating motifs. Spacing will depend on the effect you want and the size of the motifs. To assure a regular placement, however—after you've given the floor two coats of a suitable ground—you will have to establish some guidelines on the floor by penciling marks along a line to locate the center of each design. Start stenciling at the far side of the room and work backward toward a door.

A more difficult design to stencil is one that is composed of either running patterns alone or these combined with a motif

OPPOSITE AND BELOW *Running borders on these stenciled floors form a diamond pattern to greet visitors. Often small medallions were stenciled in a different color where the lines intersect to give the pattern more visual interest.*

centered within each of the areas. Particular attention must be given to measuring where a running design is used. If these dominant lines are allowed to converge, however slightly, after you begin stenciling, you will reach the near side of the room and find you are combating unexpected intersections or areas that have become too small. Then how are you going to stencil in your motifs?

One way to approach the problem is to cut running patterns in long sections—the longer the better—but not so long as to be awkward to handle. This will help guarantee straighter lines. Lay this pattern on the floor first and stencil the entire floor with it. When it is dry, go back and insert your motifs. Another method is to cut the diagonals *and* the motifs into one large square of stencil material. Then you can paint in the cutouts with different colors concurrently before lifting and moving the stencil over to another space. This is trickier unless you have measured accurately, for you don't want to end up on the near side of the room with only a partial pattern.

No matter what design you choose, after the paint dries and you have allowed the patterns to age for a few weeks, apply two coats of sealer. This will preserve your work and make it appear as though it had been there forever.

A Portfolio
of Stencil Designs

This appendix contains traditional designs that may be used to inspire your own creativity. Most have been reduced by half. To restore them to their original size, redraw them onto 1/4-inch graph paper or use a photocopier to enlarge them. The latter method, of course, will save time and frustration and probably be more accurate.

Once you have the reproduced image in the proper scale (or in any scale that most suits your wall stenciling project), do a little measuring, make your cutouts on stencil material, gather your materials, roll up your sleeves, and get to work.

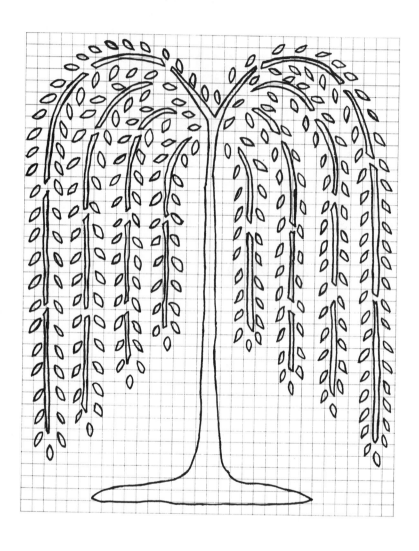

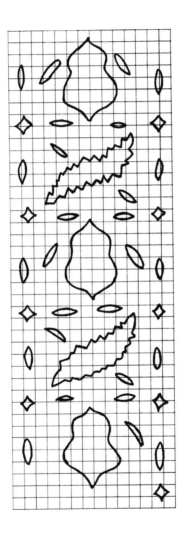

PART I OF THE COMPOSITE ACANTHUS FRIEZE DESIGN.

PART II OF THE COMPOSITE ACANTHUS FRIEZE DESIGN.

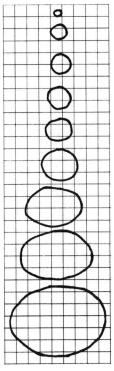

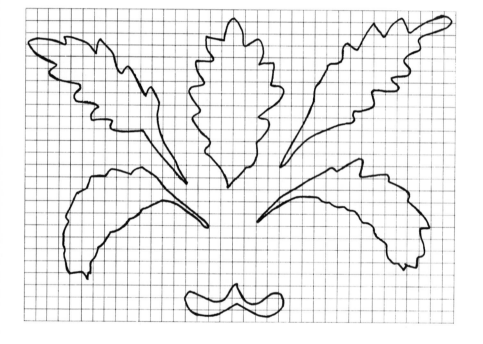

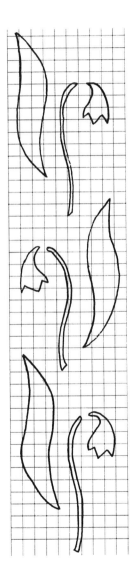

PART I OF A COMPOSITE DESIGN.

PART II OF A COMPOSITE DESIGN.

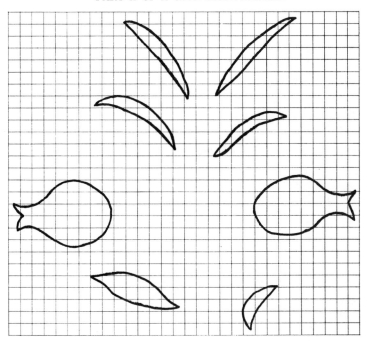

PART I OF A COMPOSITE MOTIF.

PART II OF A COMPOSITE MOTIF.

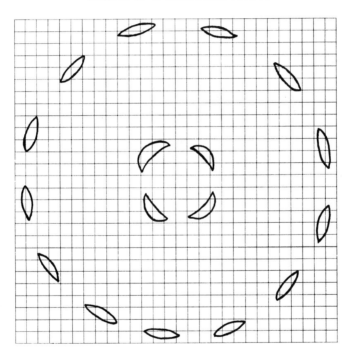

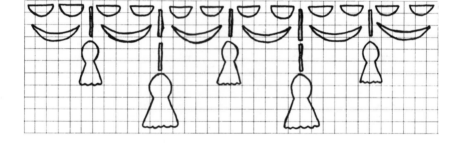

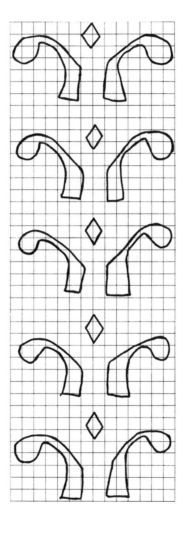

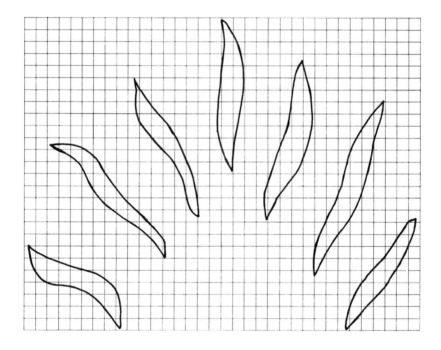

PART I OF A COMPOSITE PINEAPPLE DESIGN.

PART II OF A COMPOSITE PINEAPPLE DESIGN.

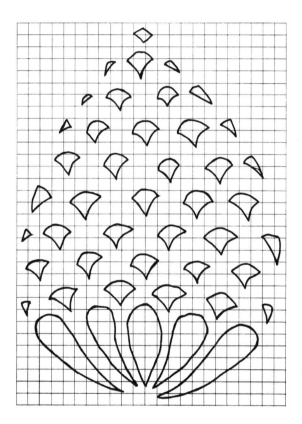

ALTERNATING PANEL MOTIF: TANSY.

ALTERNATING PANEL MOTIF: BEEBALM.

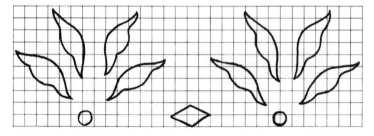

FRIEZE.

RUNNING BORDER: SWEET WOODRUFF.

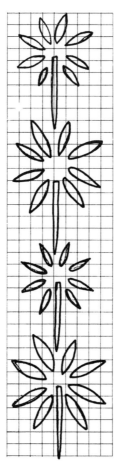

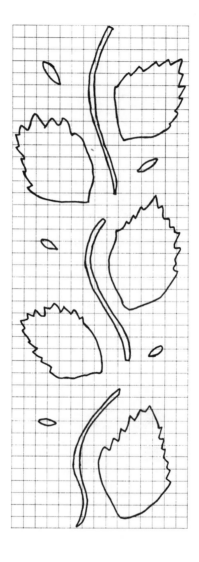

Further Reading

When this book appeared in its original edition, the few books and many articles that had been written on the subject were all directed toward the historical evolution of wall stenciling rather than toward its practical application. These were scholarly landmarks in the field of American decorative wall and floor treatment and should be consulted by anyone interested in this kind of domestic art. In addition to providing background information, they also include innumerable photographs that can be used for inspiration.

Little, Nina Fletcher. *American Decorative Wall Painting (1700–1850)*. E.P. Dutton Co., New York, N.Y. Although the stress here is on wall painting, the book also includes photographs and discussions on wall stencil patterns of historical interest for today's student.

————.*Floor Coverings in New England Before 1850*. Old Sturbridge Booklet Series, 1967. This small paperback includes a large section of pictures stressing floor covering of all kinds. Many photographs are of early American portraits in which domestic decoration can be studied. An ample bibliography of articles written on various aspects of the subject can lead to further investigation.

Waring, Janet. *Early American Stencils on Walls and Furniture*. Dover Press, New York, N.Y. This is the most comprehensive and earliest work on the subject of wall stenciling. To compile it Waring devoted decades of her life photographing extant walls (many of which have long since fallen into decay) and researching their origin. Publication of this scholarly work established Waring as the leading authority in this field of American decorative art.